From Persecution to the
Promised Land

Pastor M El Masih

WESTBOW
PRESS®
A DIVISION OF THOMAS NELSON
& ZONDERVAN

WestBow Press books may be ordered through booksellers or by contacting:

WestBow Press
A Division of Thomas Nelson & Zondervan
1663 Liberty Drive
Bloomington, IN 47403
www.westbowpress.com
1 (866) 928-1240

ISBN: 978-1-9736-0771-7 (sc)
ISBN: 978-1-9736-0773-1 (hc)
ISBN: 978-1-9736-0772-4 (e)

Library of Congress Control Number: 2017917443

Print information available on the last page.

WestBow Press rev. date: 12/06/2017

CONTENTS

FOREWORD

I have known Pastor M El Masih for many years in my capacity as a pastor, a professor, a missionary, and as a board member of Cry of the Persecuted Church. It is in all of these capacities that I wholeheartedly recommend this book to you. Pastor Masih is an acknowledged expert on the plight of the persecuted church around the world, as well as leading authority in the United States on Islam. He is an author, a preacher, a teacher, a missionary, and a man mightily used by God both in this country and abroad. I personally know of few who have sacrificed more that others might hear the truth that will set them free, and few who God uses more powerfully on a daily basis.

His own story of persecution as a pastor in his native Pakistan and escape to the United States is both inspiring and encouraging. God miraculously intervened numerous times to lead him where He wanted him to go. Pastor Masih arrived in the United States in 1999 and began immediately to spread the good news that God loves Muslims, but also that Islam has an agenda different than is popularly presented in the media. My own church has been powerfully blessed by hearing his testimony, by his careful teaching on Islam, and on how loving Christians can more effectively reach Muslims with the gospel. I have also heard him teach persuasively on a variety of other subjects, including prayer, spiritual warfare, personal revival, evangelism, the Holy Spirit, facing persecution, and living by faith. We have traveled together in several South Central Asian countries, where I have seen God continually use him in amazing ways.

I am so pleased that Pastor Masih's testimony is now available in print, presented almost as if he is giving it to you verbally himself. I have heard his testimony several times, but never heard all the details, until I read this book. It has been a rare blessing for me to now learn the entire story, and I couldn't recommend it more wholeheartedly to you.

A former president of Voice of the Martyrs ministry told me, "Pastor Masih has not only a miraculous testimony and a mighty message, but also a marvelous ministry of speaking the truth in love." Would that someone might say that about me!

Kent Mathews, MDiv, ThD, PhD
Board of Directors, Cry of the Persecuted Church

PREFACE

My dear brothers and sisters, in this book you will read stories that I hope will build your faith—encouraging you to believe more confidently in the Lord Jesus Christ and to trust more passionately that with God all things are possible. You will also read stories about persecution; some of it is persecution that I experienced myself. Through it all, Jesus was with me; he never left me, even in the most difficult of circumstances. As I reflect on His presence during those times, I am reminded of the poem "Footprints in the Sand":

> My precious child, I love you and will never leave you;
> Never, ever, during your trials and testing.
> When you saw only one set of footprints,
> It was then that I carried you.

It wonderfully expresses Jesus's continuing presence with us. There were times when He carried me in His arms because I could not carry myself. As I look back on those times, I am reminded of Psalm 23:4 (KJV):"Even though I walk through the valley of the shadow of death, I fear no evil; for Thou art with me."

I can personally testify that persecution is difficult—very difficult—and can be very painful. But God allows it in order to fulfill His plan and purpose in our lives. He uses it to test us, that we might be approved, that we might become vessels of honor and mighty weapons in His hands, and that we might become instruments for His glory.

I often say, without a test you cannot have a testimony: No test, no testimony! Or: No cross, no crown! No crucifixion, no resurrection! No burial, no eternal life! Persecution is designed for the Christians, not to destroy them, but to build them up, so that they might become mighty warriors for God. He has used persecution to spread the Gospel and to save lives around the world—spiritually, and sometimes physically.

Think about Joseph. He was persecuted by his brothers and thrown into a pit. From that pit, he was sold as a slave and sent to Egypt. There again, he was persecuted and thrown into prison. Because God was with him, he was taken from the prison to the palace! He became second in command to Pharaoh. And through him, God saved many other lives, despite enduring much persecution in his own life. The stories of Shadrach, Meshach, Abednego, and Daniel tell of persecution that ultimately led to victory. They endured the persecution; then came the promotion! I often say persecution brings promotion.

We are told in the New Testament that God used persecution to spread the Gospel throughout the world. Similarly, if I had not been persecuted, you would not have this book in your hands. But because of that persecution, God took a man like me, from a small village in Pakistan, and has used me to touch the lives of people I would otherwise not be able to reach. And as I continue to trust Him, God continues to open more doors of opportunity. Jesus himself endured persecution, making the ultimate sacrifice that brought eternal life. He said, "Remember the word that I spoke to you, 'A slave is not greater than his master.' If they persecuted Me, they will also persecute you; if they kept My word, they will also keep yours" (John 15:20 HCSB).

It is an honor to be persecuted for His name's sake. In the middle of my own persecution, I have discovered I am so much more aware of God's presence and feel so much closer to Him. I have learned that the church grows in the midst of persecution, though persecution is not the reason the church grows. It is because people pray and fast more; they depend on God more, and, as a result, the church grows. No matter what the setback, as a follower of Jesus Christ, we never lose! When we live for Jesus, even if we are persecuted, or even die, we do not lose: We win, win, win! We win big!

As I learned to trust in Jesus, He made a way where there was no way—again and again! He continues to make a way, to clear a path or open a door. As you read, I trust that you too will be encouraged to trust Him, that He will never leave you nor forsake you, and that no matter what happens, whether you live or die, He will be with you.

This book also contains stories of miracles, healings, dreams, and visions. For some of you, this may be unsettling. You may have been taught that God does not move as He did when Jesus walked on the earth, and that He does not speak anymore. Please do not close this book because you have not experienced this for yourself. God continues to do mighty miracles. Millions of Muslims, and those of other faiths, are coming to know Jesus Christ through dreams and visions. I believe that as you read the pages of this book, your perception will be expanded; you will be reminded that Jesus Christ is the same yesterday, today, and forever. Many of the things He did two thousand years ago, He is still doing today.

I have included in this book much of my teaching about Islam, thus providing information to help you understand that Allah and Jehovah God are not the same; and to understand more about Jihad and the role of women in Islam. But most importantly, you will learn how you might pray more effectively for Muslims—that they might come to saving faith in Christ—and how you might more courageously reach out to them.

As I have journeyed with the Lord Jesus Christ since March 14, 1993, I have become increasingly aware of the necessity for prayer and fasting to empower us to live victoriously. As we read the pages of Scripture, we discover that Jesus's life modeled for us the power of living in constant communication with the Father. And so I have included teachings on prayer and fasting, on praying for the lost, and on praying for those in authority.

I will be sharing my dreams and visions that the Lord has given me about the endtimes and about judgment on the United States in another book, titled *Dreams and Visions*. I pray that this will not frighten you or put you off. I believe that God can use them to bring you awareness. He loves us so much. He wants us to pray and fast, and to intercede for our nation. As you will read here, the Scripture tells us of many situations in which God was about to bring judgment upon the people.

But someone, or some group, fasted and prayed. God heard their prayers and intervened, delaying His judgment or changing it.

> For God so [greatly] loved and dearly prized the world, that He [even] gave His [One and] only begotten Son, so that whoever believes and trusts in Him [as Savior] shall not perish, but have eternal life. For God did not send the Son into the world to judge and condemn the world [that is, to initiate the final judgment of the world], but that the world might be saved through Him. (John 3:16–17 AMP)

ACKNOWLEDGMENTS

I thank God the Father, who sought after me and found me, saved me, and made me His child. I thank God the Son, who suffered and died to pay the penalty for my sins, and who daily sends his angels to guard and protect me. And I thank God the Holy Spirit, my very beloved and sweet friend, who supports, encourages, comforts, and instructs me, and without whose guidance I could not have written this book.

I thank God for my beloved wife, Esther, who, like Queen Esther of old, has fasted and prayed many times over many years for me and my ministry, stood with me through the most difficult of times, and been my faithful partner in life and in ministry.

I thank God for my parents, who opened their home to the missionary team that brought the Gospel of Jesus Christ to me.

I thank God for my two beautiful daughters, Joy and Jessica. My story is also their story, because they suffered with me from their earliest years.

I thank God for my wonderful teacher and mentor Daniel Scot, without whose help my own teaching on Islam would remain less developed. In this book most of the teaching on Islam is provided by Daniel Scot.

I thank God for my very dear sister, Jan Turner, and her husband, Leonard. Jan has encouraged me in prayer, and for years has managed various administrative aspects of my ministry. But most importantly, she helped interpret this story. She took my testimony and teachings, and transcribed them with great care. This book has been made possible through her patient participation over more than five years. Jan, you are a treasure. I thank God for all you are and all you have done.

I thank God for my dear, beloved brother, Pastor/Doctor Kent Mathews, and his dear family. They have stood with me, my family, and the ministry when the challenges were the greatest, even when it seemed impossible for me to continue in the ministry. My brother Kent has suffered with me, and comforted and supported me when I was in the greatest time of need and felt the most alone.

I thank God for Dan and Lori Singleton, my passionate partners in ministry and prayer. And for Dan's sister, Jodie Alvis, who provided considerable proofreading assistance.

I also want to say thank you to many church pastors, ministry leaders, and Christian brothers and sisters who have endorsed me on my YouTube channel—*Cry of the Persecuted Church*.

Finally, I thank God for my many brothers and sisters across the United States and around the world who encourage our ministry. So many people have done so much to help so many others—it is humbling, and families in the United States have given, truly sacrificially, to support our ministry outreaches. We are so grateful for those who have supported our overseas ministries, whether through adopting a pastor and his family, providing support for the medical clinic, funds to help schoolchildren, leadership training or other outreach projects. Special thanks to the families and individuals who have sacrificed in order to contribute financially, enabling us to free families from enslavement in the brick kilns of Pakistan, and to provide housing and the means for establishing small businesses to support their families. May God bless and protect you mightily.

INTRODUCTION

Ramadan is the month during which Muslims believe that their prophet Mohammed was visited by the angel Gabriel. In their tradition, they believe that Gabriel imparted to Mohammed the words of the Qur'an, the holy book of Islam. Ramadan is a thirty-day fast for Muslims. Historically, it is a time when many Christians and Jews have been persecuted. During Ramadan, Muslims fast during the daylight hours. They do not eat, drink, or have sexual intimacy during the daytime. They read one section (of the thirty sections) of the Qur'an each day, so that the whole Qur'an is read during Ramadan. The last night of Ramadan is known as the night of power, when they believe that Allah hears their prayers. Muslims also believe that their "righteous" deeds become more powerful that night.

It was just after 8:00 a.m. on February 6, the last day of Ramadan 1997. As I walked in the courtyard of my friend's home, I felt the refreshing breeze and reflected on a beautiful time spent in prayer, followed by a delicious breakfast. The quiet of the early morning filled the air.

Suddenly and violently, the peace was shattered as I heard gunshots and screams. The screams seemed to be coming from everywhere, and were growing louder and louder. It did not take long to realize that the screams were coming from mobs of angry Muslims. They were racing through the streets calling for the death of Christians. Over and over again, I heard "Kill the Christians! Burn their homes! Destroy their churches! Allahu Akbar (Allah is greater)."

Though I lived only a few miles away, I had stayed at my friend's home following a church gathering the night before. His home was surrounded by a wall and had a courtyard. A man came bursting through the gate, his eyes wide with fear. He was also Christian and told us that Shanti Nagar, my town, was burning. He said, "The town is destroyed. All the Christians have been slaughtered!" My heart was filled with terror and grief. My first thought was of my wife and children. I was very thankful as I remembered that she was still in Lahore recovering from the birth of our second daughter a few days earlier. I learned from her later that after they learned of the attacks, they began trying to contact me and could not find me. It was a terrifying time for all of us.

As I began to realize what was happening, I remembered that the name Shanti Nagar means "Jerusalem or City of Peace." Our peace had been stolen! Our Jerusalem was burning. The scripture from Nehemiah (1:3b–4a NASB) came to my mind, "The wall of Jerusalem is broken down and its gates are burned with fire … when I heard these words, I sat down and wept and mourned for days."

The sounds of violence grew louder, and I realized there was no time to sit and weep. I peeked into the street and saw masses of Muslims rampaging through the streets, destroying homes and businesses. My friends and I realized we were in grave danger. We fell to our knees and began to pray. We cried out to God in a whisper, "Lord, if today is our day to die, please help us to be faithful, even unto death. We do not want to deny you."

We decided we would try to escape through the back wall and go down an alleyway. The chaos in the main street was increasing as we carefully made our way outside of the town to a mustard field. The mustard plant grows as high as seven feet tall in Pakistan. We made our way to the center of the field and hid among the plants. What a contrast between the pleasant smell of the yellow mustard flower and the suffocating smoke of the burning villages.

The newspaper articles and reports from that day estimated from thirty thousand to seventy thousand Muslims rioted against the town of Shanti Nagar and the surrounding villages. The line of Muslims marching on the village stretched out for five miles in one direction and a mile in another direction. Complete chaos was in the streets. Shanti

Nagar and surrounding Christian villages were in flames. Cattle and livestock were burned alive. Farms and fields were set on fire. Vehicles were destroyed. The local medical center, the schools, and all the church buildings were burned to the ground. Men, women, and children ran for their lives. Women who were pregnant were fleeing as quickly as they could run; some gave birth along the way. Approximately two hundred women were raped. The babies born had no clothes, and the weather was cold at that time of year. Approximately fifteen hundred homes and thirteen church buildings were burned during the attacks. None of the victims had insurance for their homes, farms, businesses, vehicles, or personal property. The Christians of Shanti Nagar and the surrounding villages lost everything they had in three hours.

CHAPTER 1

Growing Up in Pakistan

When I was growing up, I attended a government school. Because the Pakistani government is run by Muslims, the government school is an Islamic school. It does not matter whether children come from Muslim, Christian, or Hindu homes; as students in the government schools, they are expected to study the Qur'an. Let me clarify that. Pakistani students do not actually study the Qur'an, but rather read it. Muslims do not really have studies of the Qur'an, nor do they believe that it should be studied—rather it should only be read and recited. As a student in the government school, I was also told that I needed to read the Qur'an in Arabic because Muslims believe that because it was originally written in Arabic, the only way to truly understand their holy book and to be rewarded by Allah is to read it in Arabic. I was born into a nominally Christian family, but I was beaten into reading and reciting the Qur'an.

Interestingly, there are about 1.6 billion Muslims in the world today. Only 20 to 25 percent of them are able to read, write, and speak Arabic. The rest of them are forced to read the Qur'an in Arabic. As a result, the 75 to 80 percent who do not really know Arabic do not understand what they are reading.

The reality is that if Muslims were able to read the Qur'an in their own native languages, many would not continue to follow the Islamic faith. If they could understand what is written in the Qur'an, they would learn of the violence, the Jihad, the killing of Jews and Christians, and even encouraging followers to hate their neighbors if

1

they are not Muslims. The intense hatred of the "infidel" (all who are not Muslim) is right there in the Islamic holy book, the Qur'an.

We often hear through the media and from politicians that Islam is not really a violent religion. It is further stated that there are just a radical few who are twisting the teachings of the Qur'an. We are told that violence and Jihad are not actually in the Qur'an. We are encouraged to believe that Islam is really a peaceful religion and that the Qur'an is really a peaceful book.

Let me emphasize here that foundational to ISIS, Al Qaeda, Hamas, and all the other Islamic groups are the teachings of the Qur'an and Hadith (historical writings about Mohammed). To call these groups "radical" suggests that there are those that are not radical. It is so important that we understand that all true followers of Islam are "radical" in that the Qur'an advocates violence against all infidels. The Qur'an teaches that if followers fight (against the infidels) for the cause of Islam, their sins will be forgiven and Allah will be pleased (Surah 3:195). And, if they die in Jihad, they will go to paradise. In paradise, every Muslim man who becomes a martyr for Allah will receive seventy-two virgins as wives (Hadith Tirmidhi 1067).

I was born in the central region of Pakistan. As a child, I was told that we were Christians, but I had very little idea about what that meant. Our family was very, very poor. There were reasons for our poverty. My father had nine acres of land. I later learned that if you have three or four acres of land in Pakistan, you can have a really good life living off the land. If someone works really hard on his land, raising cotton and wheat, he can produce enough food to feed his own family and livestock, as well as having additional produce to sell to other families. I know that many people in Pakistan worked very hard on their two- to three-acre farms, and later, purchased more land because of the money they earned by the hard work. In other words, with their hard work, they were able to sell some of their produce so that they could eventually purchase additional land.

Following my time in the military, and after teaching, I worked on my own farm. When I was teaching, I had soft hands and feet, and my body was not very muscular or strong. But, when I began working on those 2½ acres, I developed blisters on my hands and feet; my skin became darkened by the sun, and I really worked hard day and night. Just before entering the ministry, I heard a sermon about tithing. I prayed to God that if He was true to His Word, even though I didn't really know anything about farming, if He would guide me, I would give my tithes to the church. And He blessed me ten times more than the farmers around me, and protected my crops from insects and disease!

When I was a child, my mother often fought with my father. Usually the arguments started because she was telling him to work. I hate to say this, but my father was not a hard-working person. He almost never worked. Sometimes he rented out his land, satisfied to survive on the rental income. He often borrowed money, using the property as collateral. When the time came to repay the loan, he would not have the money and so would sell off a small portion of the property. This cycle repeated itself until he no longer had any land.

My parents went to the Christian church sometimes, but there was no fruit in their lives. My father never expressed any affection toward us. He never prayed with us, or even prayed at all that I saw. He only read the Bible to himself, but did not share a verse with us or encourage us to read the Word of God. He did not speak words of affirmation to us. Though my mother was not as distant as my father, she clearly favored her youngest son, and then her oldest son. I was one of the children in between and felt neglected. I remember often going to school barefoot because I had no shoes to wear.

I do have some memories of childhood fun. There were sand dunes about a half mile from our town. Some of my happiest moments during my second-, third- and fourth-grade years were going to the sand dunes with my friends after school, climbing to the top and rolling down to the bottom, doing it over and over again. We had so much fun playing there. But when I went back home, I would sometimes be beaten because my hair was full of sand, and my clothes were dirty.

In the summer months before my sixth-grade year, a Christian outreach team came to our village. We had a big courtyard at our home, and my parents agreed to host the services each evening. It was exciting to have people come from another area. I really noticed and was attracted by the love of our visitors. I eagerly volunteered to help them by bringing water and food as they needed it. During the evening services, I listened to the gospel presentation as though hearing it for the first time. The message of Jesus's love and forgiveness touched my heart. When given the invitation, I prayed to receive Jesus into my heart and promised to follow Him. Joy filled my soul, and I was baptized that week. It was a good summer, and for the next two months, I found myself reading the Bible, praying and attending church services. I was very enthusiastic about my faith. However, despite my enthusiasm, I had no foundation of Bible knowledge, and no discipleship to help me build on that foundation.

When I returned to school in the fall for the sixth grade, I had a very cruel teacher. He was a devout Muslim and forced us to memorize parts of the Qur'an. He was easier on the Muslim students, and, of course, it was easier for them to memorize the verses because they already knew Quranic verses. My native language is Punjabi, and Urdu is my national language. I also knew Hindi, learned through the movies we watched from "Bollywood" in India. The Qur'an is written in Arabic, and Muslims believe that it must be read only in the original language. That was very difficult for those of us from Christian families. For the first month of that year, my teacher beat me with a big bamboo stick every day! I tried so hard to memorize the assigned verses because I hated the beatings. Someone told me that there was a Muslim family that would help me with the memorization. For four months, this family tutored me. When I would go to the family, I had to ceremonially wash my hands before touching the Qur'an, and say the creed of Islam many times. In English, the creed is "There is no god but Allah and Mohammed is Allah's apostle." According to Islamic faith, if someone says the creed of Islam, that person becomes Muslim. Thankfully, I improved on the memorization, and the beatings stopped!

The more I learned about Mohammed, the more attracted I was to Islam. And even at the age of eleven, I could see that Muslims in Pakistan had respect and positions of power, but as Christians we were second-class citizens. When I read the story of how Mohammed had married a six-year-old girl, I began to fantasize what that would be like. I would talk with my friends, and we would imagine how enjoyable it would be to be able to marry like that. That led us to begin having lustful thoughts. And we began fantasizing about the girls in our neighborhoods. Because girls and boys were separated in our schools, we had little opportunity to interact with the girls.

Please understand that Mohammed described the scenes of paradise so graphically in the Qur'an and Hadith that it was like hearing of an orgy or watching a pornographic movie. As an example, it describes young girls standing in line and waiting for their turn to have sex with one man—one who had become a martyr for Allah.

During that time I thought a lot about converting to Islam, but decided against it because it would have brought shame upon my family. Though I didn't convert to Islam at that time, I was no longer interested in my Christian faith. I no longer had a desire to study the Bible. Instead, I began to take my Islamic studies more seriously. I continued to study Islam more intentionally throughout my school years.

In the summer months (sixth-, seventh- and eighth-grade years) we would occasionally go to a big water canal near our town. It was almost like a river. The water was brown because sometimes the cows and water buffalos were in the same water. It was quite deep, six to eight feet and we swam in that canal. We really liked to go to the area where the trees were overhanging the water. We would climb the trees and jump into the water. That was during the months of June and July, when the temperature normally goes up to 110 to 120 degrees. It wasn't until much later that we learned that sewage was dumped into that same canal. We would get out of the water and roll ourselves in a powder kind of dirt that was very hot. If you had seen us then, you might have thought you were seeing demons! After rolling in the dust, we would jump in again! It was such a fun time. However, I paid a steep price for the moments of fun. When I returned home, I was often beaten by my parents.

During this same time frame, another favorite activity was when my friends and I would take our homemade slingshots and shoot birds, or at least try to. Once again, a beating was usually waiting for me when I returned home.

CHAPTER 2

New Shoes, Chores, and Early College Days

I remember when I bought my first pair of leather shoes. Because my father rarely worked, I went without shoes for much of my childhood. My uncle had three sons, the oldest of which was almost the age of my father. My cousin was very hard-working. He sold milk and eggs. His son was the same age and grade as me. When I was ten or eleven, he offered me a job sometime in August. I went with his son at 4:00 to 6:00 a.m. every day to sell eggs, and continued in that job until December. My cousin told me that for every egg I sold, I would get 2.5 paisa. One dollar is equal to one hundred rupees, and one rupee is equal to one hundred paisa. In other words, when I sold forty eggs, I received one penny. That is poverty! Just two days before Christmas, we went to the big city and visited a shoe store called Bata Shoes. That is a very well-known company in that part of the world. For the very first time, I purchased leather shoes with the 65 rupees I had earned and saved. I was so excited and happy. I can still see those shoes. The memory is imprinted on my internal hard drive!

My father had two cows and one water buffalo. My daily after-school chores included going into the fields. The fields did not belong to us, but to strangers. I was supposed to pull the weeds and the grass from the crops, and we would gather the grass and weeds (almost 150 pounds), pile it on our heads and carry it back home (a distance of one to two miles). We would take it to a neighbor's place, where we would feed the long grass into a shredder (in Urdu we would call it a *toka*) to chop it for feed for the cows and the buffalo. It would be almost eight in the evening before I finished feeding the grass to the animals, giving them fresh water, and sometimes bathing them. It was very difficult and hard work, and it was also demeaning, considering that my father had once owned the land, but did not work to produce from it. Because of all of this, people looked down on us. We were not well-respected in our community, and it was just because my father would not work. His refusal to work created much suffering for the rest of us.

As a teenager, when the three months of summer vacation came, I worked with construction crews in our area. It was very hard work, using hammers to crush stones that were used in mixing concrete and for roadbeds and home foundations. We worked nine or ten hours a day, six days a week. I earned the equivalent of about twenty-five to thirty cents a day (equal to 25-30 rupees)! With the money I earned, I paid my school fees and purchased my textbooks for the next school year. Without the job, I would not have been able to attend school.

After eight in the evening on school nights, I would do my homework and study. Most of the time, I would be up until midnight with my school work. Often the electric power was not working, so I would have to study by the light of a kerosene lamp. I can still smell the smoke and remember the black soot that would collect in my nose! And, I didn't even have a comfortable chair to sit on while I studied. We had one steel chair, which was straight-backed. I would sit on that straight chair for the four hours of study. Sometimes, the steel felt so cold, but that helped me to stay awake! I had such a deep desire for an education that I persisted though I was uncomfortable and tired. The hard work paid off because I was able to remain at the top of my class throughout my years of school.

After completing high school, I went to college. I worked during the summer vacations so that I could purchase my textbooks and pay for my other needs. I remember I rode a bicycle to college, about seven miles each way. My father had the bicycle, which he bought from a Muslim man named Mohammed Hanif. The bike was used when he bought it. My father used the bike for a long time, and then my older brother used the same bicycle. I remember that the bicycle had so many spots where it had welding repairs. We could not even afford a new bicycle, we were so poor. By the time I began riding that bike to college, it must have been almost twenty years old!

I remember one day as I was in a first-year college class, the professor announced that if anyone could not afford to pay his or her college fees, there was a grant available through the Zakat Fund, which is one of the pillars of Islam (giving alms). Those funds were to be used only for Muslims, not for any non-Muslims. But, because I changed my name to an Islamic name when I was in my final grade in high school, I was able to qualify for the grant. I had changed my name at the encouragement of my high school English teacher. As I was completing the paperwork for the final exams, he emphasized (though he was a cultural/nominal Christian) that if I put my given Christian name, I would be looked down upon and persecuted. And, more importantly, that name would be my official government identity. He encouraged me to apply with a Muslim name, also suggesting that I would have a much greater chance to advance through college. By this time I had little regard for Christianity. I was attracted by Islam, and I had a future to be concerned about, so I agreed to his suggestion.

I did not tell my family or Christian community that I had taken an Islamic name. Because of the persecution in Pakistan, many Christians are now giving their children Islamic names rather than Biblical/Christian names to avoid physical, financial, and social persecution. This began a double life for me. When I was with Muslims, I was a Muslim, and when I was with Christians, I was a Christian. In later years, when my family and friends found that I had changed my name, they did not question it because many Christians in Pakistan live this double life to avoid the bigotry and persecution. It is very typical for Christians doing business with Muslims to hide their Christian identity by using Muslim greetings and Muslim names.

I was accepted to college for that fall. I studied premed, as I desired to become a doctor. With a Muslim identity, and as a good student, I continued to excel in college. As I look back, I realize how God allowed my college fee to be paid by the Islamic treasury. It reminds me of the story of Moses, who was raised in Pharaoh's home, ate at his table, and was educated at his expense. Later, when God found him, He used the same Moses who had been raised by the Pharaoh, to lead the people out of Egypt. He even wrote the first five books of the Bible!

It was as if God was repeating that same story. Once I was educated by Muslim funding, and now I am exposing their lies. When I reflect on those things, I regret my double life as a nominal Christian (acting like a Christian when among them) while pretending to be Muslim when with the Muslims. But today, I am so grateful that God allowed all that happened to me, although it was not His perfect will for my life. My prayer is that my story will be a help, encouragement, and challenge to those who are living a double life.

CHAPTER 3

A Father Wound and Nominal Christianity

My father's absence in my life—even though he was physically there every day—led to a deep anger that I buried because I could not openly express it. The anger began to eat me up inside. I was a very angry teenager looking for ways to stop the pain. The lack of guidance from my father left me vulnerable to all kinds of sin. *I ask you, as a reader of this book, if you are a father, please do not neglect your child, because the wounds you are inflicting on the soul of your child will continue to impact his/her life until he/she experiences Jesus's healing touch.*

During my early years in college, I was exposed to pornographic films that were not even supposed to exist in my country. We would rent a TV, video player, and video, carry them back to the college dining hall and watch them together. Those films exposed us to almost every kind of sin that you might name. Beyond that, those films rekindled the sexual stimulation that had begun years before as we listened to Mohammed's descriptions of the orgy-like environment of paradise.

In Pakistan you do not see adult stores, bars, liquor stores, or casinos lining city streets. But all of these things are there, available in the black market. I discovered through a Google search that despite the fact that pornographic films are produced here in the United States, Pakistan is listed as the number one country for hits on porn sites! According to the research carried out by PornMD, six out of the top ten countries worldwide that watch the most porn are Muslim countries. The results were based on information provided by the countries themselves.

The exposure to pornographic materials is a contributing factor to a life filled with guilt and shame for the nominal Pakistani Christian. Let me share something about the culture of Pakistan. It may help you to understand the kind of environment in which I was raised.

In Islam, shame is a major factor, and guilt is ignored. The guilt eats you from the inside, like a cancer. But you must keep your secrets hidden because of shame. Hypocrisy is a big part of the Muslim society. There are many "nominal" Christians in Pakistan, some believing that because they were born into Christian families, they are Christian. However, if you look at their lives in the light of God's Word, there is no fruit, and no difference between them and the Muslims, though they call themselves Christian. They are ashamed of their faith in front of Muslims, but when they are with the other nominal Christians, they are ashamed to leave their faith.

In Muslim countries such as Pakistan, if you are a non-Muslim, for the most part, you cannot own or operate a store or shop because no one will do business with you. When those who call themselves Christian do business in the shops owned by Muslims, they sometimes hide their faith because they are afraid of the persecution that would come if they professed their faith in front of the Muslims. So they pretend to be Muslim. In Pakistan, for the most part, Christians are segregated from Muslim society. Muslims live in the good areas, while Christians live in the lower-class areas.

Many nominal Christians are caught between two worlds. When they go to work, they face the Muslim societies, where they have decided it is advantageous to hide their faith. Returning home in the evenings, they gather with other nominal Christians. They are also experiencing guilt and shame but are unwilling to expose and confess their sins and be free. The majority of Christians in Pakistan live this kind of double life.

Though they selectively profess their Christian faith, their lives bear little fruit. Further, they are not encouraging one another to stand strong in their faith, and they are not maturing as followers of Christ.

The "double" life of the nominal Christian is a common thing. I am reminded of James 1:6–8 (NKJV), "But let him ask in faith, with no doubting, for he who doubts, is like a wave of the sea driven and tossed by the wind. For let not that man suppose that he will receive anything from the Lord; he is a double-minded man, unstable in all his ways."

The life of a nominal Christian is a horrible, horrible life. Why is it so prevalent and why does it continue? Christians in Pakistan are very, very poor, living far below the poverty line. Most of them make only forty to fifty dollars per month. Many of them are uneducated because they cannot afford to go to school. The Islamic culture has also become a part of their daily lives. In that culture, the elders, fathers, and uncles are always right, even if they are dead wrong. As a child, you have no say. You only do what is expected of you. You are expected to do things for the elders, but you do not receive any gratitude in return. Affirmation spoken into the lives of children is almost nonexistent. Growing up in such an environment does not provide the understanding of individual choice. So the bondage continues.

CHAPTER 4

Serving in the Pakistani Army

After my premed studies, I decided to leave college and enter the armed forces. I had three reasons for entering the military. First, because I already had a college education, I would enter as an officer. I had already learned that Christians are second-class citizens and are persecuted for their faith. Because I came from a nominally Christian family, I determined that Christianity offered me nothing. I chose the military, thinking that as an officer, I would gain the status, honor, and respect in society that I so desired. The second reason I chose the military was that I would have an opportunity to pursue my medical education, and the government would pay for it. And the third reason I chose to join the military was that from grade one through college, I had been taught that if I became a Muslim, and I died in Jihad against the infidels, my sins would be forgiven, and I would go to paradise and have seventy-two virgins. Even though I did not fully understand what that meant, it was very appealing to me. In college I had done two years of training with the Pakistani National Guard, which prepared me for entering the military. It also prepared me for service in case of a national emergency. And I received twenty college credits for participating.

As an officer, I had two soldiers assigned to me as servants. They were expected to shine my shoes, wash my clothes, make my bed, wait on me in the dining room, and drive me wherever I needed to go. It was like a dream come true! I had come from extreme poverty, but as a military officer, I had status, respect, and servants! What a great job that was to me! And, though I did not have a "death wish," I was hopeful that if I died in Jihad, Allah would indeed be pleased, and I would receive the promised rewards for my willing sacrifice. **But God had a different plan for my life!**

Second Timothy 2:13 (ESV): "If we are faithless, He remains faithful; He cannot deny Himself." I had all but forgotten that I had prayed to receive Christ when I was eleven years old. I had walked away from my faith in Jesus by turning to Islam. But, praise God! He had not walked away from me. On the last day of my military training, I had to take an exam. Muslims get up early in the morning, between four and five o'clock, for prayers. On that morning, I was alone in my room as I prepared for the test. All of a sudden I heard an audible voice say, "This is not the place for you. This job will lead to your destruction." Somehow, though I did not recognize it to be the voice of Jesus at the time, the voice shook me, and I was very disturbed. It was later that I realized it had been the voice of Jesus that I heard. I knew that destruction meant Hell. Confused, I prayed about the military. "Oh God, if this is not your will for me to be here in the military, then please take me out of this place." I could not shake that voice echoing in my spirit. I cried out and Jehovah God, the God of the Holy Bible, heard my prayer and took me out of there. At that time I had no idea of the differences between the God of the Holy Bible and Allah, the god of the Qur'an. I did not know that it was Jehovah God working in the situation, but here is how He moved me out of the military.

There were eighty questions on the final exam for completion of officer training. I was shaking inside when I entered the exam room. I had always been a good student. And I knew the questions because I had studied well. The second question on the exam was written unclearly. I decided to skip it, move on to the rest of the questions, and come back to that one at the end. The answers to the test were on a computerized scan sheet. Little did I know at the time, but I began to put each answer in the wrong column. In other words, I put the answer for question #3 where the answer to #2 should have gone. Every answer after that was in the wrong place. By the time I came to the last question, there was no time remaining to review the test. Consequently, I failed my military exam. I was told that I could repeat the exam. But as the voice I had heard continued to echo in my spirit, I knew I was not to continue in the military. And so I was dismissed.

I have since learned that Yahweh is the great name of God. There are so many religions in the world, but Yahweh has not allowed them to use the name Yahweh in their religious books. In the Qur'an, you will not find the name Yahweh. In the books of the Hindu religion, you will not find the name Yahweh. It is the unique and blessed name of the only true God. I praise the Lord for that. In Exodus 3:15 (NLT), God spoke to Moses from the burning bush, "Say this to the people of Israel: Yahweh, the God of your ancestors—the God of Abraham, the God of Isaac, the God of Jacob—has sent me to you. This is my eternal name, my name to remember for all generations." And in Exodus 6:2–3 (NLT), we read "And God said to Moses, 'I am Yahweh—the Lord.' I appeared to Abraham, to Isaac, and to Jacob as El-Shaddai—God Almighty—but I did not reveal my name, Yahweh, to them."

Though I did not even know Him, I believed the God of the Bible had taken me out of the military. But I was afraid when I gave up my position as an officer. It was the same fear I had felt when I gave up the pursuit of a medical career. At first, I did not even tell anyone. I did not want to tell anyone that I had failed the test. I certainly did not want to tell anyone that I had heard an audible voice. I was afraid that they would think that I had lost my mind because I was hearing voices. So, I simply returned to college and completed my studies to become a teacher.

I studied two years at the University of Multan, majoring in chemistry. I still had a desire to serve in the military. And, I still heard that voice echoing in my head. I tried to put the voice of God out of my mind. Things about military life were very attractive: paradise for martyrs, the respect of others, a good salary, good housing, and a special school for military children. I was hopeful that I could still be accepted back into the military. But God had a different plan for my life. Praise the Lord!

CHAPTER 5

Desperation and Lack of Peace Lead Me to Jesus

After I finished my studies, I found a teaching job at an Islamic high school in Karachi. I was a man without peace. Desperation filled my soul. I taught for just six months at that school. Then I took another teaching position. The desperation and lack of peace continued to bother me, and I quit that job too. I changed teaching jobs four times and finally decided that teaching must not be the career for me.

I did enjoy music very much. I began performing as a singer with a musical group. We quickly became popular and kept busy playing for weddings, parties, and religious events. One day I sang for a religious ceremony at a demonic shrine. There was a religious leader, actually a witch doctor, there. The people were honoring him because they believed that he had many powers. This man was casting out demons and sending the demons into other people. As I sang, the people washed the feet of the witch doctor. The water was black with filth and grime. The people believed this water was holy and blessed because it came from the spiritual leader. They began to drink the dirty water and to wash their faces and bodies with it. The atmosphere was so oppressive it made my skin crawl. While I sang and observed this demonic worship, the same voice I had heard three years before spoke to me. The voice told me that I should immediately leave and if I kept performing with the group, my life would be destroyed. I finished the song and told the band that I was done and needed to leave. We were being paid well, and the band wanted me to come back the next day. I told everyone that I was through.

It was not just my band members that wanted me to stay. The witch doctor also wanted me to stay and to continue coming back because my singing appeased his demons. He threatened that he would use his demonic powers to bring me to him so that I could continue to sing at his shrine. I told him that the God who told me to leave would protect me, so I was not afraid.

I moved back to my home village. My soul was dark with hatred. At one point, I found out that a local family was stealing water from our small farm. I plotted to kill the whole family. I took a gun and hid near the spot where they had been stealing the water. They did not come out that day. I now know that God protected me, for I would have been put into prison for their murders. This incident was an example of the rage that was in my heart. I was a man wandering, and my life was without peace.

During this time some Christians befriended me. They learned of my love for music, and we began learning from each other. They were going on a retreat and asked if I would like to come along and play music with them. I decided to go. It was March 14, 1993. That evening a pastor came to my room and shared the Gospel of the Lord Jesus Christ with me. My heart was stirred when I read Matthew 11:28–30 (NIV): Jesus said "Come to me, all you who are weary and burdened, and I will give you rest. Take my yoke upon you and learn from me, for I am gentle and humble in heart, and you will find rest for your souls. For my yoke is easy and my burden is light." I thank God for sending Pastor Umer Deen to my room that night. I finally knew where the voice that had been echoing in my spirit had come from. Jesus found me there and filled me with His Spirit.

That night I was so happy, and I was also very sad. I wept. I was experiencing happiness and sadness at the same time, and I cried for hours. I was happy because Jesus found me that night, and He saved my life. I was sad as I thought about all the years I had wasted without

Jesus. I had turned my back on Him so quickly after I had accepted Him when I was eleven.

But the next morning I felt like a new person, changed by the power of the gospel of Jesus Christ and His salvation. I had a deep hunger to read His Word. Even though I didn't understand it, I finally knew peace, that peace that I had desperately wanted for so long.

The writers of the Qur'an and the Hadith say that they follow the true god. But, there is no assurance of salvation in Islam. You will not find anywhere in the Qur'an or the Hadith, which are the words and teachings of Mohammad, where he says "I can grant you or assure you of eternal life." In fact, when he was on his deathbed, he told his family and friends, and his beloved daughter Fatima, "You can have my property, but I cannot save you from damnation and the hellfire." On another occasion, Mohammad said, "Although I am the apostle of Allah, I do not know what Allah will do to me." (See appendix 4).

But in the Bible, Jesus said, "Let not your heart be troubled: ye believe in God, believe also in me. In My father's house there are many mansions: If that were not so, I would have told you" (John 14:1–2a KJV). Jesus further assures us that He is going to prepare a place for us, and then He will return here and take us back with Him (John 14:2b–4 KJV). "I go and prepare a place for you. And if I go and prepare a place for you, I will come again, and receive you unto myself; that where I am, there ye may be also. And where I go ye know, and the way ye know." And remember that when the disciple Thomas asked how that could be since they did not know the way to where He was going, Jesus responded with, "I am the Way, and the Truth, and the Life. No man cometh unto the Father, but by me" (John 14:6 KJV). *My dear brothers and sisters, Jesus Christ is the only way to heaven!*

Overnight, I had become a person full of Jesus and His joy and love. I wanted to tell everyone about this Jesus, who had changed my life, and filled me with His love and joy. I was not afraid to die because I knew where I would go when I died. I did not yet really know anything about the Bible, but I knew that Jesus had saved my soul. In time I would discover that He is the Resurrection and the Life (John 11:25 KJV). He is the Way, the Truth, and the Life (John 14:6 KJV). He is the Living Water (John 4:10–11 KJV). He is the Bread of Life (John 6:35 KJV). Jesus said, "I am He who lives, and was dead, and behold I am alive forevermore! Amen. And I have the keys of Hades and death" (Revelation 1:18 KJV). Jesus also said, "And I tell you that you are Peter, and on this rock I will build My church, and the gates of Hades shall not prevail against it" (Matthew 16:18 MEV). John 8:36 (NKJV) records these words of Jesus, "Therefore if the Son makes you free, you shall be free indeed."

I knew my life had changed. I knew that I had been freed from the power of Death and Hell. I would later learn that my name had been written in the Lamb's Book of Life. "He who overcomes shall be clothed in white garments, and I will not blot out his name from the Book of Life; but I will confess his name before My Father and before His angels" (Revelation 3:5 DARBY). Praise the Lord and glory to the Lamb of God who took away my sins, set me free, and paid my debt in full. Hallelujah!

Over six million Muslims are becoming Christians in Islamic countries every year. I am often told that Islam is the fastest growing religion in the world. That is not true! I was in a meeting where a Muslim was also in attendance. He was boasting that Islam is the fastest growing religion in the world. While the Qur'an says that Muslim men can have as many as four wives, the Bible says that a Christian man is to be the husband of one wife. It is clear that with four wives, a Muslim man is likely to have more children than a Christian man. So when they say that Islam is the fastest-growing religion in the world, it is important to realize that the growth is through birth rate, not through conversion. But, praise the Lord! Christianity is growing through conversions at a greater growth rate than Islam. Sometimes people think that if more people are following a religion, it must be the true religion. That is what I believed before I became a true Christian, and that was my downfall, leading me to believe that Islam was the true religion. Christians in Pakistan are in the minority. But we see a great example when we look to the great flood. Only Noah and his family were saved in that day.

"Then the Lord said to Noah, 'Enter the ark, you and all your household, for you alone I have seen to be righteous before Me in this time'" (Genesis 7:1 NASB).

Even in the teaching of Jesus, He said,

"Enter through the narrow gate; for the gate is wide and the way is broad that leads to destruction, and there are many who enter through it. For the gate is small and the way is narrow that leads to life, and there are few who find it" (Matthew 7:13–14 NASB).

"For many are called, but few are chosen" (Matthew 22:14 NASB).

"And He spoke many things to them in parables, saying, "Behold, the sower went out to sow; and as he sowed, some seeds fell beside the road, and the birds came and ate them up. Others fell on the rocky places, where they did not have much soil; and immediately they sprang up, because they had no depth of soil. But when the sun had risen, they were scorched; and because they had no root, they withered away. Others fell among the thorns, and the thorns came up and choked them out. And others fell on the good soil and yielded a crop, some a hundredfold, some sixty, and some thirty." (Matthew 13:3–8 NASB). Note that only an estimated 25 percent of the seed sown yielded a crop.

When we turn again to the Old Testament, we find in Genesis 18 and 19 the story of Sodom and Gomorrah. Genesis 18:20 (NASB) tells us, "And the Lord said, 'The outcry of Sodom and Gomorrah is indeed great, and their sin is exceedingly grave.'" Sodom and Gomorrah were cities, home to hundreds of people. Only three, Lot and his two daughters, escaped the storm of fire and brimstone which fell from heaven.

God's Word tells us that He does not want anyone to perish, that He wants all to be saved. John 3:16–17 (NASB) makes it so clear: "For God so loved the world, that He gave His only begotten Son, that whoever believes in Him shall not perish, but have eternal life. For God did not send the Son into the world to judge the world, but that the world might be saved through Him."

God's love for us is so great. His compassion is overwhelming, and His mercies are new every morning. Yet He also warns us not to just hear the Word, and then fail to do it:

"But prove yourselves doers of the word, and not merely hearers who delude themselves. For if anyone is a hearer of the word and not a doer, he is like a man who looks at his natural face in a mirror; for once he has looked at himself and gone away, he has immediately forgotten what kind of person he was. But one who looks intently at the perfect law, the law of liberty, and abides by it, not having become a forgetful hearer but an effectual doer, this man will be blessed in what he does" (James 1:22–25 NASB).

As I said, over six million Muslims are becoming Christians every year. Over 70 percent of them are becoming Christian, not because they have a Bible or have heard the preaching of a pastor, but because Jesus Christ Himself is visiting them in dreams and visions, and they are hearing His voice. Hallelujah! Thank You, Lord!

CHAPTER 6

Following Jesus and Overcoming Temptation

Let me share something with you. Sometimes we think that once we give our lives to Jesus, everything will be good, rosy, and pleasant. We consider that the devil will no longer have access to us; that is, if we even have an understanding that there are evil forces at work in the world. We read in Matthew 4 that after Jesus was baptized by John, He was led by the Holy Spirit into the wilderness. There He fasted for forty days and forty nights. The devil came and tempted Jesus, and Jesus overcame all the attempts of the enemy by the Word of God. Every time the devil tempted Jesus to do something, Jesus replied, "It is written in God's Word ..."

> Then Jesus was led up by the Spirit into the wilderness to be tempted by the devil. And when He had fasted forty days and forty nights, afterward He was hungry. Now when the tempter came to Him, he said, "If You are the Son of God, command that these stones become bread."But He answered and said, "**It is written**, 'Man shall not live by bread alone, but by every word that proceeds from the mouth of God.'" Then the devil took Him up into the holy city, set Him on the pinnacle of the temple, and said to Him, "If You are the Son of

God, throw Yourself down. For **it is written**: 'He shall give His angels charge over you,' and, 'In their hands they shall bear you up, lest you dash your foot against a stone.'" Jesus said to him, "**It is written** again, 'You shall not tempt the LORD your God.'" Again, the devil took Him up on an exceedingly high mountain, and showed Him all the kingdoms of the world and their glory. And he said to Him, "All these things I will give You if You will fall down and worship me." Then Jesus said to him, "Away with you Satan! For **it is written**, "You shall worship the LORD your God, and Him only you shall serve." (Matthew 4:1–10 NKJV, emphasis is mine)

After I was saved, the devil tried to intimidate me and bring fear into my life. Almost every night I had a recurring nightmare. In that nightmare, I began to hear the sound of music, and then I saw a woman at a distance. After a while, I would begin to feel like a heavy weight had been placed on my chest. In my nightmare I was trying to call for help, and to call out the name of Jesus. It was so difficult. In that nightmare, with all my strength I managed to cry out, "Jesus, help me." Then quickly the weight was removed from my chest.

That nightmare pattern repeated itself for weeks. I was very exhausted by the nightmare, and I felt very angry. One night I began to pray, and Jesus appeared to me. I asked Jesus, "Why are you not removing this demon from me? Why are you allowing this demon to torment or oppress me?" I had thought that since I was a born-again Christian, the devil would not torment or oppress me. So, I asked Jesus, "Why?" And, Jesus put into my heart that I should read from His Word where He said to His disciples, "Behold, I give you the authority to trample on serpents and scorpions, and over all the power of the enemy, and nothing shall by any means hurt you" (Luke 10:19 NKJV). Then Jesus showed me some other passages from His Word. Psalm 91:11–12 (NKJV) says, "For He shall give His angels charge over you, to keep you in all your ways. In their hands they shall bear you up, lest you dash your foot against a stone." I read in Daniel 10:21 (NLT): "Meanwhile,

I will tell you what is written in the Book of Truth. (No one helps me against these spirit princes except Michael, your spirit prince)." What wonderful assurances that the Lord is faithful to send help!

And then Jesus showed me from His word that he has given me the authority over all demons and devils. Now, I need to be rebuking and telling the devil to leave. He already won the victory for me on the cross and has given me the authority. Now this is my battle, and I can use the authority which He has given to me through His name, through His blood and through the Word of God. I must command this demon, in His name, to stop tormenting and oppressing me.

After Jesus showed me all these things, I prayed and then commanded the demon that had been tormenting and oppressing me to reveal herself. And I saw the woman I had seen so often in my nightmares. She had once appeared to me as beautiful but was now ugly and scary. When she was standing in front of me, I asked the Lord to send His angels, and especially the Archangel Michael. I saw two angels come. One was a "normal" size, like the height of an average man. The other was very tall; his head seemed to almost touch the heavens, and his feet were on the ground. I knew in my spirit that the bigger and taller angel was the Archangel Michael, and the other was a "regular" angel which God had sent. I told those angels to grab the demon, in the name of Jesus Christ, and lock her up in a dungeon so that she would never be able to torment me again. I saw the small angel just grab her hair and begin to drag her. The demon was screaming, begging, and promising, "I promise I will not torment you again. Please don't let them take me away and lock me up." But I knew the devil was the father of lies. I did not listen to anything she was saying, and I didn't show any mercy. Satan is not worthy, nor are his demons worthy, of any mercy. The Bible says, "Blessed are the merciful, For they shall obtain mercy" (Matthew 5:7 NKJV). Satan has no mercy for anyone, so he cannot receive mercy.

As people of God, we should not listen to the devil and his demons, and should not make any compromise because there is no union between God's people and Satan. Praise God! Almost twenty-four years have passed since that time, and I have never had another nightmare like that or experienced the torment and oppression. Now when I think about demons, I remember that they have no authority over my life. As I stand in the truth that they have no authority, and I have been given authority over demons through the Word of God, then I remember they are powerless in my life. It is not my power but with the power that is in the Name of the Lord Jesus Christ, His blood, and His Word.

Many times we think, we might even have been told, that by simply saying a salvation prayer with a pastor, all of our problems will be solved. What we do not realize is that for all of our lives, until we choose a relationship with Jesus Christ and are born again, we lived independently of God—following the devil, being influenced by him and his demons, as well as the world and our own flesh. Satan does not leave us easily when we choose a relationship with Jesus Christ. He will continue to harass, tempt, accuse, condemn, and deceive us. It is so important that we have mature Christians disciple us, teaching us how to study the Word of God and walk in its truths, how to pray effectively and discern the voice of God, to discover and know who we are in Jesus Christ, and to understand, then exercise the authority He has given us through His Name, His blood, and His Word. Part of our discipleship journey can certainly be an experience like I had where Jesus came and taught me directly. The more time we spend in prayer and in His Word, the more we learn to discern His voice and the more we realize that He is always available to us, the more we can expect those one-on-one encounters where He responds to our prayer, takes our hand, and guides us into His truth. Hallelujah!

One day I was thinking about Jesus Christ being the only way to heaven, and considering why He is the Son of God. On that day, the Lord spoke a very profound word to me. Why is Jesus the Son of God? It is not only because He was born of the Holy Spirit. It is not because He performed many miracles. We find the complete answer when we read Romans 1:1–4 (KJV): "Paul, a servant of Christ Jesus, called to be an apostle, separated unto the Gospel of God (which he had promised afore by his prophets in the Holy Scriptures), Concerning His Son Jesus Christ our Lord, which was made of the seed of David according to the flesh; And declared to be the Son of God with power, according to the spirit of holiness, by the resurrection from the dead." Hallelujah! This is indeed the answer! Jesus is the Son of God because He was resurrected from the dead—the only one to overcome death and the grave! In order to be a giver of eternal life, the person must first conquer death. Jesus had to overcome death, and because He did, He is the only One who can give us eternal life! Hallelujah! I was reminded again of when Jesus had instructed me to command the demon to stop tormenting and oppressing me.

CHAPTER 7

First Taste of Persecution and Called to Preach

As I began to understand the Truth of the Gospel, the Lord then gave me the desire to go share with others. I did not know what was involved in preaching and teaching. I just wanted to tell people that Jesus saves and that Jesus sets the captives free! I remember that in my early, early days of preaching, I saw a friend. We had gone to school together. I shared with him what I learned about the hope and life I had found in Christ. He repented of his sins and asked Jesus Christ into his heart as we prayed together!

What joy filled my heart! When my friend returned home that evening, he told his family about his new faith in Jesus. His father sent word, inviting me to come to their home. He wanted to talk to me about what I had shared with his son. They lived out in the country in a large home with many rooms, and with lots of farm animals. I remember that as I walked to their home, I felt so much joy. My friend had come to Christ, and his father wanted to talk to me. I was sure that his whole family wanted to receive Christ!

When I arrived, the father answered the door, invited me in, and then led me into their back room. He then locked the door behind me, took a large, thick stick, and began to beat me. Then he angrily announced, "Now call on your God to come and rescue you!" He screamed at me, "I am more powerful than your God. Where is your

God now?" Though I did not fight back as he beat me, I did cry because of the stinging pain of each blow to my legs, my back, and my rear. I was covered with lashes and bruises as he continued the beating. "Call on your God to come and rescue you. I want to see if He will come and protect you."

This was my first experience being beaten for the name of Jesus. I thought of Jesus on the cross crying out in pain and asking the Father to forgive His enemies. Though it seemed like hours, after a few minutes of beating, the rest of his family heard the commotion and began banging on the door telling the man to stop. He finally stopped the beating, opened the door, and told me to leave. I told him that I did not hold anything against him but, rather, that I forgave him. I had read the words of Jesus in Luke 6:27–28 (NASB): "But I say to you who hear, love your enemies, do good to those who hate you, bless those who curse you, pray for those who mistreat you." As I left I prayed, "Father, forgive him, for he doesn't know what he is doing." Though I did not see this man again, I later learned that two of his sons died at very young ages and a third son was tormented by evil spirits. The two sons and daughter who accepted Jesus were well.

I had chosen to truly surrender to Jesus Christ as my Savior and Lord. I rejoiced in knowing Him and realizing all that He did for me. But I will admit that I became very discouraged. I thought, "This is a very dangerous job to share the Gospel. I shouldn't be doing this thing." But, the Lord impressed upon my heart that this was my calling, to preach the gospel. Initially, I responded to the Lord by explaining to Him that I would sing the songs, go to church every Sunday, or direct the choir, but that I didn't really want to be a preacher because it was clearly a very dangerous job! When I went to church the following Sunday, the pastor was preaching the story of Jonah, the prophet from the Old Testament. He talked about how God had called Jonah to go to Nineveh to preach to the people there.

"Arise, go to Nineveh, that great city, and cry out against it; for their wickedness has come up before Me." But Jonah arose to flee to Tarshish from the presence of the LORD" (Jonah 1:2–3a NKJV).

"But the LORD sent out a great wind on the sea, and there was a mighty tempest on the sea, so that the ship was about to be broken up" (Jonah 1:4 NKJV).

"Now the LORD had prepared a great fish to swallow Jonah. And Jonah was in the belly of the fish three days and three nights" (Jonah 1:17 NKJV).

"So the LORD spoke to the fish, and it vomited Jonah onto dry land" (Jonah 2:10 NKJV).

"Now the word of the LORD came to Jonah the second time, saying, 'Arise, go to Nineveh, that great city, and preach to it the message that I tell you.' So Jonah arose and went to Nineveh, according to the word of the LORD" (Jonah 3:1–3a NKJV).

I was so frightened by that sermon! I knew that that sermon was for me, even though I did not like hearing it! And, I was greatly convicted. I knew that if I ran away from my calling, the outcome would be worse than what I anticipated would happen if I became a preacher. Somehow, I understood that I should obey God's call. In Matthew 10:28 (NKJV), it says, "And do not fear those who kill the body, but cannot kill the soul; but rather fear Him who is able to destroy both soul and body in hell." Wow! It was amazing to learn that they could only kill my body, but they could not kill my soul. I knew that I needed to be obedient to the Lord Jesus Christ. "Okay, Lord, I will be a preacher." I was learning that disobeying God would be much worse than the persecution which might come from the Muslims or anyone else.

Remember that earlier I shared that Christians in Pakistan are second-class citizens, taking the low jobs, such as cleaning bathrooms and cleaning up for the Muslims. Many are slaves in the brick factory. They are very underpaid, often making between forty and fifty dollars per month. It is very difficult to provide for a family. As I thought about all of this, I again tried to convince God that He should change His mind about calling me to be a preacher. I reasoned with God that

I had already given up my military position, my pursuit of a medical career, and my teaching job. I questioned God: "How are you going to provide for me? One day I will have a wife and children also. How are you going to provide for all of us?"

But the Lord took me to Matthew 6:25–34 (NASB): "For this reason I say to you, do not be worried about your life, as to what you will eat or what you will drink; nor for your body, as to what you will put on. Is not life more than food and the body more than clothing? Look at the birds of the air, that they do not sow nor reap nor gather into barns, and yet your heavenly Father feeds them. Are you not worth much more than they? And who of you by being worried can add a single hour to his life? And why are you worried about clothing? Observe how the lilies of the field grow, they do not toil nor do they spin, yet I tell you that not even Solomon in all his glory clothed himself like one of these. But if God so clothes the grass of the field, which is alive today and tomorrow is thrown into the furnace, will He not much more clothe you? You of little faith? Do not worry then, saying, 'What will we eat?' or 'What will we drink?' or 'What will we wear for clothing?' For the Gentiles eagerly seek all these things; for your heavenly Father knows that you need all these things. But seek first His kingdom and His righteousness, and all these things will be added to you. So do not worry about tomorrow; for tomorrow will care for itself. Each day has enough trouble of its own."

Today, there is much talk about the weak economy, and discussions about how to resolve our financial situation. I believe Matthew 6:33 (NASB) is the best stimulus package available! "Seek first His kingdom and His righteousness, and all these things will be added to you." Americans, if you want a good economy—Mr. President, if you want a good economy—seek first the Kingdom of God and His righteousness, and all of these will be added to you! Ask Jesus to be your savior, your master. We need to seek His face. *He is the answer!*

I decided to follow Christ Jesus by faith. I had no idea how I would live, how I would eat, what I would wear. But I was truly determined that I was going to follow Jesus whether I had food or no food, clothes or no clothes, shelter or no shelter. I was called a fool by family members. I remember visiting one of my cousins in his home. He rebuked me, insulted me, and told me that I had lost my brain and that I would starve to death. He said, "Look at me! I have the same education as you. I am the director of a large organization. I have cars, servants, and a home. I have everything. But you are a fool. You have decided to follow Jesus. What is Jesus going to do for you? You are just a plain fool!" I wept as I left his home, telling him what Jesus said in His Word: "For what profit is it to a man if he gains the whole world, and loses his own soul?" (Matthew 16:26 NKJV).

As I later reflected on that encounter with my cousin, I was reminded of Paul's words in Philippians 4:11–12 (KJV): "Not that I speak in respect of want: for I have learned, in whatsoever state I am, therewith to be content. I know both how to be abased, and I know how to abound: everywhere and in all things I am instructed both to be full and to be hungry, both to abound and to suffer need."

Years later, after completing Bible College, planting churches and finally coming to the United States and beginning our ministry here, I learned that my cousin had lost everything because of his adulterous lifestyle. He no longer had his home, his cars, or his position. "For by means of a whorish woman a man is brought to a piece of bread and the adulteress will hunt for the precious life" (Proverbs 6:26 KJV). I later received a phone call from him asking for a job in our ministry there in Pakistan. When he called, I remembered his harsh words when I had visited him in his home years before. I told him that I could only hire him if he repented of his sins, accepted Jesus as His Savior, and was baptized. He did repent, accepted Jesus, and was baptized. He worked in our ministry office for several years.

This experience taught me that we should never ridicule God's people, or underestimate Him or them. We do not know when those we have ridiculed may be in a position to help us in our time of need. First Samuel 2:7–8 (NKJV) says, "The Lord makes poor and makes rich; He brings low and lifts up. He raises the poor from the dust and lifts the beggar from the ash heap, to set them among princes and make them inherit the throne of glory."

CHAPTER 8

God Opens the Door
for Bible College

The more I shared the Gospel of Jesus Christ, the more I realized that my knowledge of the Bible was limited. I wanted to go to Bible College. I went to the Lord: "God, I need to go to Bible College so that I can learn Your Word and how to share it with others."

There are two major Bible Colleges in Pakistan. One is run by the Salvation Army. The other is run by the Methodist Church, which is called the Church of Pakistan. I asked God, "God which Bible college should I attend, the Salvation Army school or the Church of Pakistan school?" God impressed on my heart that He did not want me to attend either one of them! In the back of my mind, I was hoping that God would allow me to attend one of these schools because I had heard about how the churches were supportive of the Bible College graduates when they became pastors. And then as I was praying, God showed me a vision. I saw a billboard for a Bible School. The billboard said, "Full Gospel Bible School." God gave me a vision to go to the Full Gospel Bible School. I argued with God, "I have heard about those people. They are very poor. Most of the students at that Bible school are only middle school graduates or high school dropouts. I am a university graduate, and you are telling me to attend Bible School with uneducated people. That is not fair." Then God spoke in my heart: "Who gave you the wisdom to complete your education?" I answered God, "You gave me the wisdom."

I had another question for God. "God, I was reading in Your Word in Mark 16:17–18 (NASB) where it says, 'And these signs will accompany those who have believed: In My name they will cast out demons, they will speak with new tongues; they will pick up serpents, and if they drink any deadly poison, it shall not hurt them; they will lay hands on the sick, and they will recover.' Your Word also says in the last verse of that same chapter, 'And they went out and preached everywhere, while the Lord worked with them, and confirmed the Word by the signs that followed.' Lord, if you have really called me to be a preacher of the gospel, I ask that you confirm my call by performing those signs, wonders, and miracles."

Before I began attending Bible School, I was traveling through a town. Someone told me that there was a boy, named Johnson, who was paralyzed, and asked if I could go and pray for him. I said, "Okay, I will go and pray." But, in my mind I was thinking that this was a good opportunity for me to test my calling. I prayed for the boy, and God did answer my prayer. The following day, the boy was walking! When I saw the boy walk, I was happy for him. But I confess that I had some doubts, thinking it might have just happened by chance!

Later, there was a woman in my hometown named Refit. She had been paralyzed also. I was asked to pray for her. I prayed for her, but she did not immediately begin to walk. However, a few minutes after I returned home, she came walking to my home to thank me for praying for her. She proclaimed that she was healed! But, again, the devil brought some doubts into my mind—perhaps she would have begun to walk anyway. "It wasn't really your prayers that had anything to do with her beginning to walk again."

Once, I was praying about two in the morning. My prayer room was next to the road. Someone began knocking at the door. When I opened the door, two men were standing there. They asked if I could accompany them to their home because their father was dying. Their father's name was Kheriat. I was really nervous about this situation. I thought to myself, "If he is really dying, what can I do about it?" But, the Lord spoke to my heart that I should go and that He will be with me. I told them that I would go with them, but when I arrived at their home, the situation was totally different than what they had told me. Their father was not dying; he was already dead! Just before I arrived, the medical doctor had come and told the family that nothing more could be done, that the man was dead.

When I heard that the man was dead, I thought in my heart, *There is no need for me to pray for this man.* But the Lord spoke to me, convincing me that I needed to pray over the dead man. In obedience I prayed, but the man was not raised from the dead. The Lord told me to pray a second time. I prayed, but there was no change. The Lord spoke to my heart a third time, telling me that I must pray again. But life did not return to the dead man. The Lord spoke to me a fourth time, instructing me to pray again. I prayed a fourth time, "Lord Jesus, raise this man from death to life." The dead man coughed and then opened his eyes. He then asked for a drink of water! I was very happy and told the Lord that I would not test Him anymore and that I would be a preacher of the Gospel!

I was able to find out about the Full Gospel Bible School. I learned about Pastor Yousef Daniel, from a neighboring town. He had recently graduated from that school. I went to him and told him about the "billboard" vision. I asked him if I could attend the Full Gospel Bible School. He told me that in order to attend the Bible School, I was required to be a member of his church for at least one year. I told him, "I cannot wait for one year. I need to attend Bible School this year!"

He then told me that I would not be able to attend that year because the date for submitting applications had already passed. "You cannot go this year. You will have to wait until next year."

I responded, "I will go this year because the Lord has told me to go."

I sent the application to the school, even though it was past the deadline for submitting applications. After a month or so, I heard that the Bible school was calling the student candidates in for interviews. I had not received acknowledgment that my application had been received, nor had I been contacted for an interview. But the Lord spoke to me that I should go for the interview. Again I argued with Him,

"Lord, I have not received any letter or contact from them. How can I go for an interview?" But the Lord told me that I must go for an interview. I took the bus from my town for the six-hour ride to the Full Gospel Bible School in Lahore, Pakistan.

When I arrived at the Bible School, I found out that they would only be selecting ten students for admission. I also found out that there were forty candidates, all of whom had received letters from the school requesting that they come for interviews. When the candidates learned that I had also come for an interview, but had no invitation letter, they laughed at me. They were sure that I must be stupid or crazy!

As I waited outside on the lawn of the Bible School, a man came out of his office. When I saw him and learned he was a secretary, I ran to him. I told him my name and said, "Sir, can you please find out if my name is on the list of candidates that have come for interviews. I submitted my application, but I did not receive a letter or any contact from the office."

He said, "Okay, I will find out." He went back to his office, and quickly returned to me. He told me that my name was the last name on the list. I was so relieved and thanked the Lord. My name was finally called for the interview. After just a few questions and a little dictation, the interview was done.

Together with all of the other candidates, we waited anxiously for about an hour to learn the results of the interviews. The principal appeared and read the names of the candidates who had been selected to be the students for the new school year. My name was the very first name to be called! I was in awe! My name was not even supposed to be there, and was the very last name on the list. Once again, God showed me that He is able to make a way where there seems to be no way. Again, God made clear to me that He is in control. He opens doors that no man can close, and closes doors that no man can open!

"And to the angel of the church in Philadelphia write, 'These things says He who is holy, He who is true, He who has the key of David, He who opens and no one shuts, and shuts and no one opens: I know your works. See, I have set before you an open door, and no one can shut it; for you have a little strength, have kept My word, and have not denied My name'" (Revelation 3:7–8 NKJV).

CHAPTER 9

Bible College and Marriage

I began attending the Bible School. The school provided free accommodations, including room and board, as well as free tuition and free textbooks. In addition, the school provided six hundred rupees for any additional expenses I might have. While I was studying at the school, three pastors approached me with a very interesting question: "When are you going to get married?" I knew they had daughters for whom they hoped to find mates. My answer to them was that I was not interested at that time because I was concentrating on my studies.

One day my principal asked me to remain following the class. I was very nervous because I was the president of the students. I was thinking that I must have neglected some of my duties as president. Even before he spoke, I started apologizing. He said, "Wait, and let me talk! I have a granddaughter who is a born-again Christian. She has also graduated from university. I want to ask you to pray about marrying her." I told him that I would pray and fast, and seek God's will concerning that.

I prayed for one month about marrying the principal's granddaughter. At the end of that time, God answered and showed me that this was His plan for my life. I told my principal, "I will marry your granddaughter." At that point I had not even seen her! Then I asked him, "Is it okay if I see your granddaughter?"

He said, "Sure!" He then took me to their home. When we arrived there, we were offered cool drinks, and we sat in the living room. I was nervous, and my eyes were spinning, looking around to find out from which direction my future wife would come. As I was about to take my second sip of soda, my eyes were drawn to the curtain right in front of me. The curtain was opened, and there she was! When I saw her, I was struck by her beauty. At the same time, I was very nervous. My legs were shaking, and my hands were getting sweaty! But my eyes were fixed on her. She came in and sat on the sofa across the room from me. I did not talk to her because in our culture, men and women do not talk with each other prior to marriage. Despite not talking, we were attracted to one another, and we fell in love at first sight. That was November 26, 1993.

Our first meeting was such an exciting encounter. But then I needed to return to my village to talk with my parents. In our culture, marriages are arranged by the parents. I needed to go to my parents to get their approval. I thank God that as I showed them her picture and shared the story of our meeting, they gave their approval.

Later when we were married, my wife told me that before I came to see her that first time, she had prayed and asked God if the man who was coming was His will for her life. She asked God to confirm His will by bringing the man to see her. If he did not come, then she would consider that to be God's confirmation that he was not the one. God had also shown her in a dream prior to our meeting that she would be getting married to a man from a village (she lived in the city).

Our engagement date was April 15, 1994. In June 1994, the school had two months of summer vacation. I joined Operation Mobilization for those two months. I was assigned to lead the Gospel ministry teams going to the different cities of Pakistan. A key part of our outreach was door-to-door evangelism to Muslims. During this time, I met one of my future wife's relatives. They spoke very negatively about my in-laws to be. I was very much poisoned by what they shared. So, I decided to break the engagement! I wrote a letter to my fiancée telling her of my decision, and returned the engagement ring. (In Pakistan, when a couple becomes engaged, sometimes both receive engagement rings.)

After I returned to Bible School following the mission trips of that summer, my former fiancée's mother called me, but I refused to meet with her. When my former fiancée found out that I was not going to marry her, she went before God. She told Him, "I prayed and asked you to confirm the one you had for me—that you would send him to meet me. Why did you allow this man to come and meet me if he is not the one who is to be my husband?" She remembered His Word in Matthew 1 when the angel is reassuring Joseph about marrying Mary. In the Urdu translation, the engagement of Mary and Joseph was the same as marriage. My former fiancée considered herself to already be my wife. She fasted and prayed for three days and three nights, no food or water, during the month of August (when it is so hot and humid in Pakistan). She did not tell anyone in her family that she was fasting. She continued with her regular activities and responsibilities. And she prayed and went before God. "Lord, I am his wife (as she presented His Word from Matthew 1:20 to the Lord). Please change his heart and bring him back to me."

Here I was in the Bible School, and one of my Bible teachers began teaching on marriage during the same time that she was fasting. As he taught on marriage, he began teaching from Matthew 1:19–20! He explained that Joseph was engaged to Mary, and was not married to her. But he explained that in the Jewish culture, engagement was considered equal to marriage. That is why the angel Gabriel visited Joseph and told him not to divorce her. "Then Joseph her husband, being a just man, and not willing to make her a public example, was minded to put her away privily" (Matthew 1:19 KJV). And then God spoke to my heart that I should not break my engagement because it is equal to divorcing. I called my former fiancée, apologized, and asked for her forgiveness. I also apologized to her parents. Thank God she forgave me! We were married on December 22, 1994!

CHAPTER 10

Going to South Africa for Further Studies

Just one week after our wedding, as I was eating my lunch, I received a phone call from South Africa. I was invited to attend a Bible College for further studies, together with my wife. It was such exciting and great news. Let me share how I became acquainted with the people in South Africa. Three pastors from South Africa came to teach in the Full Gospel Bible School in September 1994. My principal asked me to interpret for them, translating from English to Urdu. I told my principal that I had never translated before. He responded by reminding me that I had a bachelor's degree in journalism, and I should at least try! In Pakistan, I could read and write English, but was not able to speak English. This was a big challenge for me. I prayed and began interpreting. I stumbled a few times, but with the help of the Holy Spirit, I was able to translate their teaching. I interpreted for them for the entire month that they were teaching at the Bible school. During the last day of their visit at our school, they asked me if I would consider going to South Africa for further studies at their Bible College. I told them that if it was the will of God, He would make a way for me to attend. And, if it was not God's will, I would be content right where I was. We exchanged contact information before they left.

When I received their phone call in December, I was very happy and excited about the opportunity to pursue further studies in the

Bible College. But I was also wondering how we would get to South Africa, and where the money would come from for travel expenses, visa fees, etc. About a week later, I received an official letter of invitation delivered by two South African pastors who were visiting Pakistan. I had mixed feelings when I received the letter. I was happy to go, to have the opportunity to further my biblical studies. But, I was also sad that I had no money for travel, living, and visa expenses.

In Pakistani culture, when a woman gets married, her parents give a dowry, which are the things needed to establish a household. My wife and I decided that we should go to the Bible College. We realized that we had been offered a unique opportunity, which might not be available later in life. We decided to tell her father, my father-in-law, Nathaniel, that we did not want to receive a dowry. We asked him to consider providing money instead of the usual dowry. He agreed to give us money. We went to the South African Consulate in Islamabad, Pakistan. Our applications for visas to South Africa were denied. Our hopes for attending Bible College there were gone.

But I thank God for my wife. She was newly married and had already given up her dowry. She decided to fast and pray for three days and three nights without food or water, just like she had done when I broke our engagement. And, it was just like Esther and the Jews had done: "Go, gather together all the Jews that are present in Shushan, and fast ye for me, and neither eat nor drink three days, night or day: I also and my maidens will fast likewise; and so will I go in unto the king, which is not according to the law: and if I perish, I perish" (Esther 4:16 KJV). After the three days and nights of fasting, God ordained a meeting with the South African ambassador. We had shared our situation with the pastor who had delivered the invitation letter. We asked if he could call the South African Embassy and meet the ambassador on our behalf. The ambassador agreed to meet with Pastor Eugene and with us.

We traveled to Islamabad to the consulate, where we met with the ambassador. This time we did not stand in the long line waiting for our turn to apply for visas. Instead we were called into the ambassador's office. We did not fill out any papers for our visas. This time, the ambassador asked for our passports, and he filled out the papers for us! He then instructed his secretary to bring the visa stamp. He personally stamped our passports with the South African visas. Glory to Jesus! Not only did we not fill out any paperwork, we also did not pay any visa fees! We purchased our plane tickets and left for South Africa on February 18, 1995.

When we arrived in South Africa, having been invited there to attend the William Carey Bible School, we were uncertain because no one was there to meet us at the airport. We had never been outside of Pakistan, so were unsure what to do. We had some money, so after exchanging it into the local currency, we called a pastor. I thank God that I had the phone number of one of the pastors who had come to teach at the Bible School back in Pakistan. It was a Sunday, and he had just arrived home from church services. He said they would come to see us, and after about an hour, they arrived at the airport. Later that day they took us to the Bible School. We were surprised when we saw that the school was in the jungle. There was only one teacher and three students.

We began to question if we had made a mistake in coming all that way. We had expected a well-established Bible College, better than the one we had left in Pakistan. We wanted to do deeper study than what we had already done, but this school did not offer even the level we had already completed. We began to think that we may not have heard correctly from God. We decided that we should go back to Pakistan. The next day, another pastor came to visit. Pastor Eugene was also one of the pastors who had come to teach in our Bible School in Pakistan. We told him that we did not want to stay there, but to return to Pakistan. Thank God, he was willing to take us to his home.

The following day, he contacted friends at Covenant Bible College in Durban to see if there was any possibility that we might be able to attend there. He found out that the principal and his church had been praying for thirty days that God would open the doors for them into Muslim countries. The principal's name was Ronnie. When they learned that we were from Pakistan, they told us that we were an answer to their prayers. They also said, "Come quickly to see us at the

Covenant Bible College in Durban." When we arrived there, they told us that our tuition fee was already paid, and that our accommodation needs were also taken care of! We were rejoicing and praising God for His incredible provision.

CHAPTER 11

Baby on the Way

We settled into our lives at the Bible College in Durban. One day my wife told me that she was not feeling well. We took her to the doctor, and, after running some tests, the doctor told us that she was pregnant. She had morning sickness, and she was no longer able to attend classes at the Bible College. She told me that she wanted to return to Pakistan so that the baby could be delivered there. She wanted to be near her family during the delivery. I was actually hoping that the baby would be born in South Africa, so that we would have a child with South African citizenship.

I honored the desires of my wife and agreed with her. But I did tell her, "We are students. We don't have any money to purchase plane tickets to return home. All the money we had from the dowry payment was spent on the plane tickets to come here. But let's pray and ask God to provide." We began praying. The next day when I went to college, my principal came into my classroom and asked me to see him after the class. I went to his office and he told me that someone had sent me a check for one thousand rands. I was so happy to receive the check. When I returned home, I received a phone call from a police officer. He invited us to join him and his wife for dinner. He came to pick us up for dinner, and after a nice dinner together, he told me that God had told him to give us one thousand rands. We praised the Lord for His marvelous provision.

Let me explain that the money needed to return to Pakistan

was about twenty-five hundred rands for my wife's one-way ticket to Pakistan, plus thirty-five hundred rands for my round-trip ticket because I wanted to return to the Bible College to complete my studies after taking my wife back to Pakistan. In addition, we would need fifteen hundred rands for medical expenses for her and for the baby's delivery. Then God put in my heart the desire to hold some revival meetings while in Pakistan for the summer vacation. I determined that I would need about two thousand rands for these meetings. So, all together we needed ninety-five hundred rands. We had received two thousand so far. After a few weeks, I returned from the Bible College one day. My wife was very happy. She told me that a pastor came and gave us 2,500 rands for her one-way ticket to Pakistan. We thanked the Lord. We then needed five thousand more rands.

A week later, I received another phone call from one of the professors at the Bible College. He wanted to travel to Pakistan with us for the summer vacation, so that he could join me in the revival meetings. He said, "Let me tell you the good news. Let's go to the travel agent and book the plane tickets for you, for your wife, and for me. I have raised funds for your ticket, and also for the revival meetings." I was amazed! Now, we only needed fifteen hundred rands for the medical expenses for my wife and the baby's delivery! I received another phone call during that same week. A pastor wanted me to come and preach in his church.

We had a wonderful worship service on Sunday morning, and then the pastor took us back to the place where we were living while attending the Bible College. On the way back, the Lord began impressing upon my heart to ask the pastor about his wife. She had not been in the service that morning. Though the Lord had impressed this upon my heart, I was hesitant to ask because it seemed like an inappropriate question. Finally, we arrived where we were staying. But, before the pastor said goodbye to us, he said, "Brother, we would like you to come for supper tonight at our home." We accepted his invitation and returned to our room for the afternoon. We began to pray. We asked God why He was impressing upon our hearts to ask the pastor about his wife. We spent more than three hours just praying about the pastor and his wife. We prayed, "Lord God, please, whatever is going on with the pastor's wife, please fix it."

The pastor came that evening to take us to his home for supper. On the way, I finally asked him, "Pastor, I did not see your wife in the service this morning. Why wasn't she in the service? Was she sick or was something wrong?"

When I asked him, the pastor almost began to weep. He told me a very terrible and heartbreaking story. He shared that more than thirty-three years prior to our meeting him, he had been a Hindu. He married a Hindu woman, but soon afterward, he had become Christian. She did not convert to Christianity. He explained that was the reason she was not in the service that morning. She continued to go to the Hindu temple, while he went to church. "I have been living for the last thirty-three years as a Christian pastor with a Hindu wife."

Finally we arrived at his home. As I was sitting on the sofa, his wife sat on the sofa across from me. The Spirit of the Lord came upon me in a powerful, powerful way. I said to her, "Sister, you need to give your life to Jesus right now." When I said that, she began to weep. She accepted Christ in that very moment! Everyone began to jump and dance! The pastor was hugging me, and his children were hugging us and dancing, shouting and screaming with joy. They were telling me that they didn't know that God had sent us to the Bible College. They believed God had brought us to South Africa for their wife and mother. Then, they told me that they had learned that my wife was pregnant. "We want to have a baby shower for her." They had the shower and began to give us gifts and money. Later, when we were going to the airport, there was a procession of cars coming to say goodbye to us. More than thirty-five people, pastors with their families, came to see us off. We had more money than we had even asked God to give us!

CHAPTER 12

Jehovah Jireh Provides
Again and Again

In June 1995, we returned to Pakistan. I had two months of revival meetings during June and July. God moved with a mighty power during those meetings. Many, many people were healed, delivered from demons, and many were baptized. In August 1995, I left my wife in Pakistan and returned to South Africa to complete my studies at Covenant Bible College. (Covenant Bible College was founded by John G. Lake, who had been filled with the Holy Spirit at the Azusa Street Revival. He was called to go to Africa to start a church. He started the Apostolic Faith Mission Church.)

When I returned to South Africa to complete my studies, I knew that I would graduate before the end of the year. I would need money for a plane ticket to return to Pakistan after graduation. Whenever I received an invitation to preach from any church, whatever gift they gave me, I saved in anticipation of returning to my homeland. Whenever I spoke at a church, I would think, "Now I have this much money, and this church will give me this much money, and then I will have this much money." I began to think more about the money than anything else. There were a couple of reasons for me to think about the money. First, I was very anxious to get back to Pakistan to see my wife, and also our firstborn baby. Also, I missed my brothers and sisters and my parents very much. But God began to deal with me.

One day I was going to a church to preach, and God gave me a sermon to preach in that church. I had been thinking about the last time I had preached in that church—they had given me a certain amount of money. I began thinking about how much I would receive when I preached this time—surely it would be at least as much as the last time, if not more. I preached the sermon God had given to me. The pastor was not happy with the message at all! The church was one with a liberal theology, and the message God had given me to preach was a very conservative one. I received no love offering or financial gift that day. However, during the service, more than half of the people attending made decisions for Christ and/or were healed. The pastor was so displeased with me that he was not even willing to take me home! But thank God for those who were saved and healed. Some of them took me back to the place where I was living.

Then God showed me that I had started to trust the people for money more than I trusted Him. That is why He had taught me this lesson. I was to trust in Him alone and always. God showed me in His Word that cursed is the man that trusts in another human being. I repented of my sin in trusting man rather than God.

A week following when I repented, and a couple of weeks prior to my graduation, my principal called me into his office. He asked me when I wanted to return to Pakistan. He told me that the Bible College intended to pay for my return ticket to Pakistan. I was overwhelmed with gratitude to God for His provision yet another time.

The brother who had been hosting me for four months while I attended Bible College, just one day before I was scheduled to leave South Africa for Pakistan, told me at the dining table that evening, "My boss came to me today and told me that for the next four months, I would be receiving four hundred rands extra salary. I was reminded in my heart that I kept you in my home for four months and that God was now repaying me for hosting you in my home." I was so blessed to know that God is with me, and He causes me to be a blessing to others.

I graduated from Covenant Bible College on November 26, 1995. On November 28, I flew back to Pakistan, where I was reunited with my wife, and where I met my firstborn child, a beautiful baby girl, for the first time.

On March 8, 1996, I was officially ordained as a pastor. God began using me with the mighty power of the Holy Spirit. Many people heard the Gospel message for the very first time in their lives. Many people were being saved, many healed, and many were delivered from demon possession. With the help of the Holy Spirit, we began to plant churches. Within 1½ years, we had planted fourteen churches.

One of our main ways of doing evangelistic outreach was with a Gospel/ministry team. Every morning we took Gospel of John booklets and other gospel tracts and went into the streets. It was very dangerous and scary, but God reminded me of a scripture He had shown me when I first heard His call to preach: "And fear not them which kill the body, but are not able to kill the soul: but rather fear him which is able to destroy both soul and body in hell" (Matthew 10:28 KJV).

He also reminded me of the power of the Holy Spirit: "But ye shall receive power, after that the Holy Ghost is come upon you: and ye shall be witnesses unto me both in Jerusalem, and in all Judaea, and in Samaria, and unto the uttermost part of the earth" (Acts 1:8 KJV).

In other words, Jesus said that when the Holy Spirit comes upon us, we will receive power. And the word for power in Greek is *dunamos*, where we get the word *dynamite*. The word *witness* in Greek is *martus*, where we get the word *martyr*. When the Holy Spirit comes upon us, it does not make us cowardly or fearful. Instead the Holy Spirit empowers us like dynamite, so that we can be as strong as martyrs for Jesus.

Martyrdom is not only dying for Jesus, but also living for Him. We are living martyrs as we share His gospel in our homes, our communities, and throughout the world. A cowardly person, afraid to stand for Jesus, will not be a martyr. And a cowardly person will not become a true Christian because the Bible says in 2 Timothy 1:7 (KJV), "For God hath not given us the spirit of fear; but of power, and of love, and of a sound mind." His Word also provides a clear warning for those who choose a cowardly path: "But the fearful, and unbelieving, and the abominable, and murderers, and whoremongers, and sorcerers, and idolaters, and all liars, shall have their part in the lake which burneth with fire and brimstone: which is the second death" (Revelation 21:8 KJV).

God really has dealt with my fear of man. I am challenged and encouraged when I read the story of Stephen, who was the first martyr in the early church. As he was being stoned, Stephen saw heaven open and Jesus standing on the right hand of the Father. It is significant to note that Stephen did not see Jesus sitting on the right hand of the Father, as we see in Hebrews 1:3 (KJV), "who being the brightness of His glory and the express image of His person, and upholding all things by the word of His power, when He had by Himself purged our sins, **sat down** at the right hand of the Majesty on high."

However, let's look at Acts 7:55–56 (KJV): "But he, being full of the Holy Ghost, looked up steadfastly into heaven, and saw the glory of God, and Jesus **standing** on the right hand of God, And said, Behold, I see the heavens opened, and the Son of man **standing** on the right hand of God." Here we see that the King of Kings and the Lord of Lords is **standing** at the right hand of the Father. He is **standing** in honor of those who are laying down their lives for Him.

Just imagine if the president of a country stands for someone—that person for whom the president stands must be a much-honored person. But Jesus Christ is above all the presidents of all the nations, above all the dignitaries, military leaders, everyone in any position of power. When Stephen saw Him, Jesus was standing for him.

As you know, I have some military training. When your commander in chief stands for you, it is a huge honor. That picture of Jesus standing changed my life and increased my boldness. I was no longer afraid of death. The Bible says that nothing can separate us from his love.

> What shall we then say to these things? If God be for us, who can be against us? He that spared not his own Son, but delivered him up for us all, how shall he not with him also freely give us all things? Who shall lay any thing to the charge of God's elect? It is God that justifieth. Who is he that condemneth? It is Christ that died, yea rather, that is risen again, who is even at the

right hand of God, who also maketh intercession for us. Who shall separate us from the love of Christ? shall tribulation, or distress, or persecution, or famine, or nakedness, or peril, or sword? As it is written, For thy sake we are killed all the day long; we are accounted as sheep for the slaughter. Nay, in all these things we are more than conquerors through him that loved us. For I am persuaded, that neither death, nor life, nor angels, nor principalities, nor powers, nor things present, nor things to come, Nor height, nor depth, nor any other creature, shall be able to separate us from the love of God, which is in Christ Jesus our Lord. (Romans 8:31–39 KJV)

The writer of Hebrews (13:6) reminds us of the words written by the psalmist in 118:6 (KJV): "The Lord is on my side; I will not fear. What can man do unto me?"And, Solomon wrote in Proverbs 29:25 (KJV): "The fear of man bringeth a snare: but whoso putteth his trust in the LORD shall be safe."

So from that point on, we went to the streets of Pakistan carrying Bibles, gospels of John, and other Bible literature every morning. We walked boldly, without any fear. As we left home each morning, we knew that that day might be our last. We might not return to our homes. But we knew that if we did not return safely to our homes, we would be moving forward to our real home in heaven. And we would sing:

I have decided to follow Jesus; I have decided to follow Jesus;
I have decided to follow Jesus; No turning back, no turning back.

Tho' none go with me, I still will follow. Tho' none go with me, I still will follow.

Tho' none go with me, I still will follow; no turning back, no turning back.

My cross I'll carry, till I see Jesus; My cross I'll carry till I see Jesus.
My cross I'll carry till I see Jesus; no turning back, no turning back.

The world behind me, the cross before me. The world behind me, the cross before me.
The world behind me, the cross before me; no turning back, no turning back.

We carried heavy shoulder bags filled with the literature, one bag on each shoulder. Many of the Muslims considered that we were carrying our own deaths on our shoulders. That was true in that distributing Christian literature could have brought death to us. Followers of Christ in countries around the world have been martyred for sharing the Gospel of Jesus Christ. But we were not and are not afraid of death. I have often said, "If you are born twice, you will only die one time." And that one death is not really death because you are entering into eternal life with Jesus Christ.

CHAPTER 13

You Must Be Born Again

I want to pause here to focus on what it means to be born again. For the answer to this most important question, we turn to the Word of God:

> There was a man of the Pharisees, named Nicodemus, a ruler of the Jews: The same came to Jesus by night, and said unto him, Rabbi, we know that thou art a teacher come from God: for no man can do these miracles that thou doest, except God be with him. Jesus answered and said unto him, Verily, verily, I say unto thee, Except a man be born again, he cannot see the kingdom of God. Nicodemus saith unto him, How can a man be born when he is old? can he enter the second time into his mother's womb, and be born? Jesus answered, Verily, verily, I say unto thee, Except a man be born of water and of the Spirit, he cannot enter into the kingdom of God. That which is born of the flesh is flesh; and that which is born of the Spirit is spirit. Marvel not that I said unto thee, Ye must be born again. (John 3:1–7 KJV)

To understand this biblical term, it is necessary to understand that there are *two births*. The "first" birth is the *physical birth*, when you were born into this world from your mother and father. The "second" birth is a *spiritual birth*, which means to be born of the "Spirit" (God's Holy Spirit). Why does a person need to be born spiritually? What is a "spiritual" birth?

The Bible teaches that man is created in the image of God. God manifests Himself to mankind in the Persons of God the Father, God the Son, and God the Holy Spirit. Likewise, mankind is composed of a body, soul, and spirit. Our body is the "tent," you could say, of the soul and spirit (the body is a temporary dwelling place). Our soul is composed of the heart (to feel), the mind (to think), and the will (to decide).

Our spirit is dead in sin when we are born; that is, we are born void of God. No person is ever born with God. The only exception is the Lord Jesus Christ, Who came as God in the flesh: "And without controversy great is the mystery of godliness: God was manifest in the flesh, justified in the Spirit, seen of angels, preached unto the Gentiles, believed on in the world, received up into glory" (1 Timothy 3:16 KJV).

The Bible says that our spirits are dead in trespasses and sin: "And you hath he quickened, who were dead in trespasses and sins; Wherein in time past ye walked according to the course of this world, according to the prince of the power of the air, the spirit that now worketh in the children of disobedience" (Ephesians 2:1–2 KJV).

The unsaved person cannot understand God or His Word: "But the natural man receiveth not the things of the Spirit of God: for they are foolishness unto him: neither can he know them, because they are spiritually discerned" (1 Corinthians 2:14 KJV).

We are born physically alive, but spiritually dead. It is only when we choose to follow Jesus Christ, to enter into a personal relationship with Him, that we become spiritually alive. God never forces anyone to accept Jesus as his/her Savior. He simply offers a warm invitation to anyone who desires forgiveness of his/her sins, a relationship with Him, to be spiritually alive and to have the assurance of eternity spent with Him.

Romans 5:15 (KJV) tells us that salvation is a free gift: "But not as the offence, so also is the free gift. For if through the offence of one many be dead, much more the grace of God, and the gift by grace,

53

which is by one man, Jesus Christ, hath abounded unto many." That free gift was paid for by the precious blood of Jesus Christ: "Forasmuch as ye know that ye were not redeemed with corruptible things, as silver and gold, from your vain conversation received by tradition from your fathers; But with the precious blood of Christ, as of a lamb without blemish and without spot" (1 Peter 1:18–19 KJV). We are saved by God's grace through faith in Christ Jesus, because of the blood that He sacrificed for our sins.

Salvation is very simple—we are sinners, and Jesus is the Savior. His gift of eternal life is free. We need only to reach out and receive it. Romans 10:9–13 (KJV) spells it out very well: "That if thou shalt confess with thy mouth the Lord Jesus, and shalt believe in thine heart that God hath raised him from the dead, thou shalt be saved. For with the heart man believeth unto righteousness; and with the mouth confession is made unto salvation. For the scripture saith, Whosoever believeth on him shall not be ashamed. For there is no difference between the Jew and the Greek: for the same Lord over all is rich unto all that call upon him. For whosoever shall call upon the name of the Lord shall be saved." Galatians 3:26 (KJV) tells us that when we have confessed Him and believed in our hearts, we become part of His family: "For ye are all the children of God by faith in Christ Jesus." The Lord gave me this revelation: as Jesus was born by the power of the Holy Spirit, so we too must be born by power of the Holy Spirit in order to be the sons and daughters of God and to be a part of His kingdom.

The Word of God tells us that He does not want any of us to be lost. Second Peter 3:9b (KJV): "Not willing that any should perish but that all should come to repentance."

We can sometimes get caught up in thinking that it is complicated and that if we don't get the words just right or do things in just the right way, we won't really be saved. Note the simplicity of their words as the tax collector and the thief on the cross cried out to God:

"And the publican, standing afar off, would not lift up so much as his eyes unto heaven, but smote upon his breast, saying, 'God be merciful to me a sinner'" (Luke 18:13 KJV).

"But the other answering rebuked him, saying, Dost not thou fear

God, seeing thou art in the same condemnation? And we indeed justly; for we receive the due reward of our deeds: but this man hath done nothing amiss. And he said unto Jesus, Lord, remember me when thou comest into thy kingdom" (Luke 23:40–42 KJV).

They simply recognized Jesus for who He is, acknowledged Him, and then cried out from their hearts. Think about how amazing it is that when the thief on the cross, hanging next to Jesus, paying the price for his many crimes, cried out to Jesus, Jesus's response was, "Assuredly, I say to you, today you will be with Me in Paradise" (Luke 23:43 NKJV).

If you have not yet made a decision to accept Jesus Christ as your Savior and Lord, you can do that right now! Simply talk to Him from your heart. If it is helpful for you, you might pray something like this:

Dear Jesus, I know that I am a sinner. I believe that You are the Son of God. I believe that You died on the cross, shedding Your blood to pay for my sins. I believe that You rose from the dead on the third day, overcoming death once and for all. I ask you to forgive me of my sins, come into my heart so that I can spend eternity with You. Amen.

If you have just made a decision to accept Jesus Christ as your Savior and Lord, please tell someone! If you are already part of a church, tell your pastor or one of the elders. If you have any questions, you can also reach us on our website: www.persecutedchristians.org. If you are not part of a church, please seek out a Bible-teaching church where you can be a disciple and grow in your understanding of God's Word and His ways—and where you can discover the amazing plan He has for your life:

"For I know the thoughts that I think toward you, saith the LORD, thoughts of peace, and not of evil, to give you an expected end. Then shall ye call upon me, and ye shall go and pray unto me, and I will hearken unto you. And ye shall seek me, and find me, when ye shall search for me with all your heart" (Jeremiah 29:11–13 NASB).

CHAPTER 14

Commandos for Jesus

I remember one morning we had a team of six ready to begin distributing four thousand copies of the Gospel of John. As we gathered, we prayed and then moved out into the streets. We had named ourselves, "Commandos of Jesus." We began distributing the booklets. Within 2½ hours, we had distributed more than three thousand copies of the gospel of John in the city of Miān Channūn, Pakistan.

Then I was cornered by some Muslims. They were very mad at me. They threatened to kill me. I knew that the area we were in was an industrial area where agricultural tools and machinery were built, and there were iron smelting furnaces there also. They let me know that they planned to take me to one of the furnaces, where they would throw me in. As they were taking me there, they said, "Don't you know that this is a Muslim country? You should not be distributing this Christian literature to the Muslims. And, besides, the Bibles you are distributing here have been changed. They are corrupt. They are not real anymore. Who authorized you to do this?"

I told them, "I know this is a Muslim country, but my God, Jesus, told me to go into all the world and preach to the nations. That is the reason I am distributing the Gospel in this country because this country is part of the world. And God has called me to preach the Gospel to the whole world. You have said to me that this book, the Bible, has been changed. And that it is not real. I want to ask you a question. I would like to know if you have read this book, the Holy Bible, and have found those changes and errors. Please tell me." They said, "We have not read the Bible."

In the Muslim world, Muslims are told that the Bible is a very dangerous book. Christians have put spells or incantations on the book and anyone who touches the book or reads it will become Christian. So Muslims are very afraid to touch or read the Bible. I asked them, "If you have not read the Holy Bible, how can you say that this book has changed or is in error? My dear friends, I suggest that you read this book first. I would appreciate if you would find the changes and errors and let me know. Here is our address where you can write to us or visit us."

They responded by saying, "That makes sense." They took the Bible from me, and then they let me go! When they let me go, I was reminded of the words of Jesus Christ: "But when they deliver you up, take no thought how or what ye shall speak: for it shall be given you in that same hour what ye shall speak. For it is not ye that speak, but the Spirit of your Father which speaketh in you" (Matthew 10:19–20 KJV). When they released me, I met my team and told them the story. Together we praised the Lord and thanked Him for His protective love, and then we moved on to the next town.

This experience did not discourage us. We went to the next town and began doing the same thing, distributing the Bibles, Gospel of John booklets, and other tracts. We distributed the rest of the materials that we had with us there. As we were finishing, I saw a small mob (ten to twenty people) of Muslims running toward us. They were shouting and screaming, "Kafir! Kafir!" Kafir means blasphemer or infidel. They were carrying sticks, stones, and bricks. As they drew closer, they began hurling the objects at us, and we began to run. We were able to escape because one of our team members had been assigned to remain in the van, following along as we walked and passed out the literature. He was instructed to keep very alert, watching us carefully, as well as the surroundings. We told him to leave the door unlocked and that if there was any danger, we would climb into the car quickly. Then he was to "hit the pedal to the metal," quickly accelerating so that we could move away from the danger. It reminded us of the words of Jesus, "But when they persecute you in this city, flee ye into another" (Matthew 10:23 KJV).

Another time we were distributing literature in a different city. We had a very good time that day. We gave out many Bibles to the Muslims. God really helped us. After finishing the distribution for the day, we were returning to the place where we were staying. We had been walking, but needed to use public transportation to make the rest of the trip. We got into a taxi/van that seated about fifteen, and was already quite full. We had a little literature remaining. All of the other passengers in the van were Muslim. The Muslims began asking us questions about the literature that we were carrying in our laps.

One of the passengers was one of the people we had given literature to earlier in the day. He had read that everyone has sinned and fallen short of the glory of God and that all of the prophets have sinned—that there is no one without sin except Jesus. So they began questioning us about Adam, Abraham, David, and all the others, asking if they had all sinned. They declared, "We believe they were innocent." (See appendix 1, "Concept of Sin in Islam.")

"You are spreading lies," they said. They were not as concerned that we were saying that all of these people were sinners, but rather that we were suggesting that Mohammed was a sinner too. They became so angry at us. They threatened to take us to the police station to be arrested the next time the van stopped. As we approached the next stop, we thanked God that we were sitting very close to the back door of the van. When the van began to slow down as it approached the station, we jumped out the back door while it was still moving. We ran as fast as we could and were able to escape. Praise God!

No Muslim, no one, can touch you unless God allows it. I have said this often. Jesus loves me, and He showed that love on the cross. But one day, when He calls me home, that will be a part of His extreme love for me. One follower of Christ, a Russian evangelist, put it this way when he was arrested by the communist police. He was told that he would be going to jail because of preaching the Gospel. "I will be very glad to go to jail because I am going to preach to the prisoners." Then the police told him they would not put him in with the other prisoners, but would put him in solitary confinement. "That will be even better because I can spend time with the Lord Jesus Christ." Then the police said, "We're going to kill you." The preacher said, "That will be the best. I will be with Jesus in heaven."And then, the police let him go!

I remember the story of another brother in Pakistan. When Muslims attacked our town on February 6, 1997, they were going house to house looting and robbing. They were also hurting the Christian men, women, and children remaining in the homes (or forcing them to become Muslim). One of the Christian brothers was dragged from his home and brought into the town square. Two Muslim men pointed guns at him, one at his chest and one at his head. They told him to deny Jesus and become Muslim. He replied, "I cannot deny Jesus because I cannot use my tongue to deny His name. I am owned by Jesus. You can cut out my tongue, but I will not deny Jesus."

They said, "We are not going to cut out your tongue. We are going to kill you."

This Christian brother said, "Go ahead and shoot me. Do it quickly. As soon as you shoot me, I will see my Jesus face to face. Actually, you will not be hurting me. You will be doing me a favor." The two holding their guns at the Christian brother turned away and let him go!

One day we went to preach and distribute literature in another town. We had a very good time. People were taking the literature, and we had a very good response. We returned to our room after a satisfying day. We decided to return to the same area the next day. Because the response had been so positive the day before, we felt it would be good to continue the evangelistic outreach in the area. When we entered one of the shops to share the gospel with the store owner, the Muslim shop owner welcomed us into his shop. He began sharing an amazing story with us. He said that the day before he had seen us in the street. He had watched as people on both sides of the street saw us and began moving toward us to attack us. But, as the people moved close to us, they could not find us. According to this man, it appeared as though we had disappeared. We could not be seen by the angry people. At the same time, we did not even see angry crowds that day! God had blinded the eyes of those intending evil toward us. He had also caused us not to even see the threat, so that we remained unafraid. But, the Lord had allowed this man to witness the whole event.

When we heard his story, we were in awe. We praised God. It reminded us of John 8:59 (NKJV): "Then they took up stones to throw at Him; but Jesus hid Himself and went out of the temple, going through the midst of them, and so passed by." We explained to the man what God had done and how He had spared our lives. And then we shared the gospel with him. Instead of taking the literature from us, he paid us for it and served us a beverage.

Our experience with the shop owner was so encouraging to us; it made us realize again how God was going before us. He often brought encouragement as we learned of His moving in other people's lives. For example:

We learned of a Muslim priest who began reading the Bible in order to find errors in it. When he could not find any errors, he became very depressed and decided to kill himself. But, prior to committing suicide, he prayed, "If the God of the Christians is true, show up now. If the God of the Muslims is true, show up now. Otherwise, I am going to kill myself tomorrow." That night Jesus Christ came into his room and stood before him with open arms and told him, "I am the Way, the Truth, and the Life. No one can come to the Father but by me. I died for you on the cross."

Praise the Lord, this man who had been a Muslim priest, became a Christian. He told his family that he had become a Christian. His own mother was so upset that she poisoned his food in order to kill him. But, as we read in the Bible, Jesus Christ is the same yesterday, today, and forever (Hebrews 13:8).We must choose to believe and walk in that Truth. The things He did two thousand years ago, He is still doing today! Hallelujah! He said, "And if they drink any deadly thing, it shall not hurt them" (Mark 16:18 KJV). Praise the Lord! The poison did not kill our brother. The man who was once a priest in the Islamic faith is now a Christian pastor sharing the Gospel of the Lord Jesus Christ!

CHAPTER 15

His Healing Touch

One day my wife and I were going into the city to do some shopping. We were riding in a horse-drawn cart (in Urdu it is called a *tanga*). As we were riding along, we passed an oxcart. We could hear screaming coming from the cart, like someone was in pain. I asked our driver to stop and find out what was going on. We found out that there was a teenage girl on the cart. She was experiencing terrible pain, so terrible that she thought she was going to die. I immediately asked the girl's family if it would be all right with them if I prayed for their daughter. They were on their way to the doctor in the city. Her pain seemed so intense that she might actually die even before she could reach the doctor. She was jerking around, kind of like a fish out of water would flop about. The family allowed me to pray for her. Thank God! The Lord touched her, and she was healed immediately. Instead of continuing on to the doctor, they returned to their home because she was completely and totally healed!

The news spread about the girl's healing. Her father told many people in the surrounding villages and towns. One day the father contacted me and asked if I could visit his relatives in a village about fifty miles from our home. He told me that the whole family was tormented and possessed by demons. In those days, I didn't even have a bicycle for transportation. But one of the elders in the church had a motorbike. He agreed to take me. We got up very early the next morning and rode the motorbike. Oh, let me clarify—there were four of us on the motorbike! The elder drove the bike, I sat behind him, and my wife sat behind me holding our baby daughter! The roads were very dusty and rough. Because of the dust, we needed to cover our heads with cloths in an attempt to keep out some of the dust. We looked like ninjas! Without the protective covering, even your dog wouldn't recognize you when you returned home! We arrived in the village and prayed for the family. The Lord delivered all of them from their torment. All of them received Jesus Christ as their Savior and were baptized! Hallelujah!

As we returned home that day, we passed a Muslim man sitting on the side of the street with his paralyzed wife. God prompted me to ask our brother to turn the bike around so that we could go back and speak to the man. I asked him, "What is wrong with your wife? And where are you taking her?" He said his wife was paralyzed, and he was taking her to a Muslim mosque. He hoped that the Muslim holy man would pray for her and that she would be healed. "Where else have you taken her?" I asked. He began to name many shrines/mosques he had visited, but his wife had not been healed.

"Have you prayed in the name of Allah?" I asked.

He said, "Yes, but it did not work."

"Did you pray in the name of Mohammed?"

"Yes, but she became worse!" he replied.

"Have you ever heard about Jesus? (In the Qur'an, *Isa* is the name by which Jesus is known.) When He was in this world, He healed the sick, raised the dead and made the cripple walk. It is even in the Qur'an. He is alive! Do you want us to pray for your wife in the name of Jesus for her healing?"

He said, "Yes!"

Thank God my wife was with me at the time. She laid her hand on the paralyzed woman as I began to cry out loudly in the name of Jesus for his wife to walk. God had already spoken to my heart, and I knew God was going to heal her, so I prayed loudly to attract others to come and watch the power of God at work. Many people were in the street, and a crowd began to form. As we said, "Amen" the lady stood up and started to walk. Glory to the Lord Jesus, she was healed. *Jesus is still a miracle-working God!*

One time I was participating in some Christian meetings. The promotions for the meetings had included signs saying, "Jesus heals" and "Jesus sets the captives free." While there were Muslims in the area who heard about the meetings and wanted to come for prayer, they were afraid of being caught at a Christian gathering. One of the Christian sisters was a nurse working at a Muslim hospital. She approached me to ask if I would pray for one of her patients. The patient was a ten-year-old boy whose kidneys were failing. She told me that if I came, we could safely meet in her home on the hospital grounds. I confess that I had mixed feelings. I was filled with joy that the Muslims wanted me to pray for their son. I was also fearful that if he was not healed, they would become angry and begin accusing me of lying.

When I went to the Lord for guidance, He impressed upon me to go to pray for the boy and meet the family. Actually, He had put it in my heart to go and preach the Gospel! When I arrived at the nurse's home, the Muslim family was there, along with thirty of their relatives! I looked at all of them and asked, "Do you want a healing or a healer? If you want the healing, you may get sick again. But if you have a healer, you can ask him for healing anytime." They all agreed that they wanted a healer! I introduced them to Jesus, our healer, Lord and Savior. All thirty Muslim family members prayed to accept Jesus into their hearts! I then prayed for their son, and Jesus, our healer, healed him! Several other people were also healed! Hallelujah! Glory to Jesus!

I visited another city in Pakistan to distribute Bibles and share the Gospel. It had been a particularly difficult and discouraging day. Many people had rejected the offer of Bibles at a discounted price. In Pakistan, one cannot distribute free Christian literature. For example, if a Bible is fifteen dollars, we would give it for ten cents because we did not want to be accused of distributing free Bibles to Muslims. I continued to pray that the Lord would guide me to some Muslims who would want to receive the Bible and read it. As I walked along the street, the Holy Spirit directed me to cross the street and enter a shop there. With renewed enthusiasm, I entered the shop and approached the owner. I asked if he would like to receive a free Bible. He told me that his vision was very poor so he could not read the Bible, or anything else, for that matter.

I could see that he was wearing very thick glasses. I also knew that the Bible I had to give him was in very small print.

In that moment such a disappointment washed over me. But, just as quickly, the Lord encouraged my faith as He instructed me about what I should say to the man. "If you could see, would you read the Bible?"

He quickly responded, "Of course I would read the Bible if I could see."

I began to tell him about how Jesus healed and brought sight to those who were blind and that Jesus could give him sight so that he could read. "Do you want me to pray for Jesus to heal your eyes and give you sight to read?"

He said, "Yes, pray for me." I prayed for him and Jesus restored his sight immediately! This man began to excitedly rejoice. He then asked if I would pray for his family also. After I prayed, and it was time for me to leave, he paid me for the Bible with the promise that he would read it! Praise Jesus, our healer!

CHAPTER 16

Ministry Becomes a Threat

As we began our ministry, many people made decisions to follow the Lord Jesus Christ. Many were baptized. As more people began to follow Christ and were baptized, the Muslims in the area became increasingly upset. Eventually, there were false accusations filed against us, claiming that some Christians had torn the pages of the Qur'an, which is a sin against the prophet Mohammed. In Pakistan, or any other Muslim country, the law is that you cannot say anything against Islam or Mohammed, otherwise you may be killed. When the Muslims began spreading the lie that we had torn the pages of their holy book and had spoken evil things against their prophet, seventy thousand to eighty thousand Muslims and government police gathered and began attacking Shanti Nagar and a neighboring town on February 6, 1997.

When I told God that I was willing to die on that day, and asked only that He help me stand strong and not deny His name, I was reminded of Luke 9:24 (KJV): "For whosoever will save his life shall lose it: but whosoever will lose his life for my sake, the same shall save it." It is important to understand that Muslims are instructed, as they are about to kill Christians/Jews/Infidels (anyone who is not Muslim), to first ask if they want to become Muslim. Then, if they choose not to follow Islam, they are to kill them. I did not want to die, but I was willing to die for my Jesus. My prayer was simply that when they asked me, I would not deny His name.

Jesus said that when we stand for Him, He will stand for us before

His Father: "Whosoever therefore shall confess me before men, him will I confess also before my Father which is in heaven" (Matthew 10:32 KJV). He is not telling us that we should only confess His Name within the four walls of the church, or when it feels safe to do so. He is asking us to confess His Name everywhere, even if someone is threatening us with death. Speak the Truth no matter what! In the Qur'an, it is written, "Oh, Muslims, do not deny your faith in Allah. But, if you are in danger, you can say with your mouth that you are not a Muslim" (Surah 16:106). Muslims are allowed to lie, to deny their faith in circumstances that they determine to be dangerous. As followers of Jesus Christ, we are not to lie, even if our lives are in danger. That is where our trust in Him is most important.

I praise the Lord that our lives were spared on the day of the attack. We did lose everything we had, including our homes. But three days later, on Sunday morning, we had a worship service. Almost everyone in both towns, all those who had lost everything, came for the service—twenty thousand people gathered for a corporate worship service. Because I was one of the pastors in the village, I was asked to speak. Oh how I sought the Lord. What can I say to my brothers and sisters, my neighbors, family and friends who have been so devastated? The Holy Spirit led me to speak on forgiveness. The Lord instructed me to remind the Christians that we are to forgive the Muslims. Muslims are not our enemies. Satan is our enemy. I was reminded of Romans 12:19b (KJV), "Vengeance is mine; I will repay, saith the Lord." It was by far the most difficult message I had ever been instructed to give. My precious family had been abused, violated, left with no homes—with nothing. God, help me!

Praise the Lord! He went before me and poured out His anointing upon me, empowering me to speak His message. The Holy Spirit moved powerfully in the hearts of the people gathered as I spoke on the power of forgiveness. When I completed the message, I asked that everyone stand and pray that they would be able to forgive the Muslims who destroyed their lives. Everyone stood, and we prayed in unison, united in Christ.

It was a week later that I was reminded again of the Lord's words,

"Vengeance is mine; I will repay" (Romans 12:19 KJV). The news carried the story about a train that derailed. The train was filled with Muslims. More than one hundred of them were killed that day. The accident occurred in a city near Shanti Nagar. Many that were on the train that day had been among those who destroyed our communities the week before. Many Muslims believed that the derailing was an act of God!

The Bible says, "Who shall separate us from the love of Christ? Shall tribulation, or distress, or persecution, or famine, or nakedness, or peril, or sword?" (Romans 8:35 KJV). I have learned so many things because of persecution. Persecution is a great gift from our Almighty God. Persecution brings perseverance. Persecution brings power in the church. Persecution brings prayer in the churches. And persecution brings freedom for the Body of Jesus Christ—freedom from the material things, and the ultimate freedom of eternity with Him!

Let's think about Shadrach, Meshach, and Abednego. These three Jews were brought before the Babylonian king. King Nebuchadnezzar told them that he would give them one more chance to bow down before the golden image and worship it. But they would not worship any idol or other god. The king issued the order for them to be tightly bound and thrown into the furnace, which he had ordered to be heated seven times hotter than normal. But, something happened! Their bodies were not burned, their clothes were not burned. Not a single hair on their heads was burned. But there was something burned—the ropes/chains that bound them! As the king looked into the furnace, he saw them walking around free—free of the ropes that had bound them, free from any burns or fire damage. He saw something else also. There were not just the three men walking around in the furnace. A fourth one was there, who looked like the Son of God.

> There are certain Jews whom thou hast set over the affairs of the province of Babylon, Shadrach, Meshach, and Abednego; these men, O king, have not regarded thee: they serve not thy gods, nor worship the golden image which thou hast set up. Then Nebuchadnezzar

in his rage and fury commanded to bring Shadrach, Meshach, and Abednego. Then they brought these men before the king. Nebuchadnezzar spake and said unto them, Is it true, O Shadrach, Meshach, and Abednego, do not ye serve my gods, nor worship the golden image which I have set up? Now if ye be ready that at what time ye hear the sound of the cornet, flute, harp, sackbut, psaltery, and dulcimer, and all kinds of musick, ye fall down and worship the image which I have made; well: but if ye worship not, ye shall be cast the same hour into the midst of a burning fiery furnace; and who is that God that shall deliver you out of my hands? Shadrach, Meshach, and Abednego, answered and said to the king, O Nebuchadnezzar, we are not careful to answer thee in this matter. If it be so, our God whom we serve is able to deliver us from the burning fiery furnace, and he will deliver us out of thine hand, O king. But if not, be it known unto thee, O king, that we will not serve thy gods, nor worship the golden image which thou hast set up. Then was Nebuchadnezzar full of fury, and the form of his visage was changed against Shadrach, Meshach, and Abednego: therefore he spake, and commanded that they should heat the furnace one seven times more than it was wont to be heated. And he commanded the most mighty men that were in his army to bind Shadrach, Meshach, and Abednego, and to cast them into the burning fiery furnace. Then these men were bound in their coats, their hosen, and their hats, and their other garments, and were cast into the midst of the burning fiery furnace. Therefore because the king's commandment was urgent, and the furnace exceeding hot, the flames of the fire slew those men that took up Shadrach, Meshach, and Abednego. And these three men, Shadrach, Meshach, and Abednego, fell down bound into the midst of the burning fiery furnace. Then

Nebuchadnezzar the king was astonished, and rose up in haste, and spake, and said unto his counsellors, Did not we cast three men bound into the midst of the fire? They answered and said unto the king, True, O king. He answered and said, Lo, I see four men loose, walking in the midst of the fire, and they have no hurt; and the form of the fourth is like the Son of God. (Daniel 3:12–25 KJV)

Praise God! Jesus showed up! When you go into the furnace, the chains and shackles which bind you will be destroyed by the fire! Fire, the fire of the Holy Spirit, is good! The fourth man—Jesus—will meet you right in the middle of the furnace. We should be excited to go into the furnace for Jesus! When we are going through the difficult times, through the persecution, the presence of Jesus is all we need. When we are in the comfort zones of our lives, we do not feel the need of Jesus! That is the way it is here in America. We must be prepared for the suffering and the persecution. It is coming to America soon. It is right at our door, and we need to be ready for that, so that when it comes to us, we will stay strong. First Corinthians 16:13 (KJV) says, "Watch ye, stand fast in the faith, quit you like men, be strong."

We have already discovered the obedience of Shadrach, Meshach, and Abednego, their unwillingness to bow down to an idol, even at the threat of a sure and excruciatingly painful death. The rest of the story is Jesus's response to their obedience. He entered the fire with them and completely protected them from being burned. But the story does not stop there. Let's read on:

Then Nebuchadnezzar came near to the mouth of the burning fiery furnace, and spake, and said, Shadrach, Meshach, and Abednego, ye servants of the most high God, come forth, and come hither. Then Shadrach, Meshach, and Abednego, came forth of the midst of the fire. And the princes, governors, and captains, and the king's counsellors, being gathered together, saw these

69

men, upon whose bodies the fire had no power, nor was an hair of their head singed, neither were their coats changed, nor the smell of fire had passed on them. Then Nebuchadnezzar spake, and said, Blessed be the God of Shadrach, Meshach, and Abednego, who hath sent his angel, and delivered his servants that trusted in him, and have changed the king's word, and yielded their bodies, that they might not serve nor worship any god, except their own God. Therefore I make a decree, That every people, nation, and language, which speak any thing amiss against the God of Shadrach, Meshach, and Abednego, shall be cut in pieces, and their houses shall be made a dunghill: because there is no other God that can deliver after this sort. Then the king promoted Shadrach, Meshach, and Abednego, in the province of Babylon. (Daniel 3:26–30 KJV)

The obedience of Shadrach, Meshach, and Abednego not only ensured their safety, it also opened the door for the Lord to demonstrate His miraculous powers in such a way that even the king could not deny Him. And then they were promoted.

CHAPTER 17

Brief History of Pakistan

The official name of my previous country is the Islamic Republic of Pakistan. The state religion is Islam. The country of Pakistan covers about 307,374 square miles, with a population of almost two hundred million people. Approximately 97 percent of the population is Muslim. Minority religions, including Christians, comprise the other 3 percent of the total population of Pakistan. Christians and other "infidels" (non-Muslims) are considered second –class citizens.

Before 1947, Pakistan and Bangladesh were part of India. These three regions comprised a subcontinent. Together, the three countries were surrounded on three sides by oceans. According to Islamic history, Pakistani Muslims did not have freedom of religion while they were part of India. According to the Hindus in India, the Muslims in the Pakistani region did have religious freedom.

When Gandhi led the nation of India, he was not interested in dividing the country. He offered Mohammed Ali Jinnah (Muslim leader) the opportunity to be the first prime minister of India after British rule. Gandhi believed it was essential for Muslims and Hindus to join together to fight against the British. Mr. Jinnah was not supportive of the idea of the united country, rather was insistent that the Pakistani region become its own country.

More than one million people were killed in the conflict between the Hindus and Muslims which led to dividing India. It was decided that where the Muslims were in the majority in India, those areas should be given to the Muslims. It was also decided that where the Hindus were in the majority in India, those areas should be given to the Hindus. On August 14, 1947, the eastern part of India and the western part of India were given to the Muslims. These regions were first known as East Pakistan and West Pakistan. The word Pakistan is said to mean pure, and also holy land. Finally, in 1971, the region that had been known as East Pakistan, since 1947, became the country known as Bangladesh. The region previously called West Pakistan became known simply as Pakistan.

CHAPTER 18

Return to South Africa

When the attack against my town happened, my younger daughter was only four days old, and my older daughter was fifteen months old. It was a very difficult time. Some of the women actually gave birth on the day of the attack. Five months following the attack, I received a call from Covenant Bible College in South Africa, where I had studied. They had heard the stories of the persecution and the attack against our towns. They invited us to come and share our story there. They promised to provide half of the airfare needed for the four of us to travel there. So, we borrowed the rest of the travel funds needed.

My wife and daughters traveled with me to South Africa. My daughters were five months and twenty months old when we boarded the plane in Lahore (capital of the Punjab province), Pakistan, on July 10, 1997. We flew to Karachi (largest city in Pakistan, located along the Arabian Coast), and from Karachi International Airport to Dubai, UAE. We had a five- to six-hour layover in Dubai, and then boarded a plane for Johannesburg, South Africa.

We arrived in Johannesburg in the early morning, between five and six o'clock. It was the winter season. In Pakistan, June through August are the summer months. But in South Africa, June through August is the winter months. We were not well-prepared for the winter weather. When we arrived at the airport, our host family had not yet arrived to meet us. We called the host pastor in Tongaat, a city, and told him that we had arrived in Johannesburg, and were waiting for them at the airport. He had assumed that the information he had forwarded to a pastor in Johannesburg (with the understanding that the Johannesburg pastor would pick us up) had been delivered to the pastor in time to meet our flight. Instead, we waited for more than two hours in the very cold winter weather.

Finally, the Johannesburg pastor arrived to meet us, and took us to his home. We thanked God for providing us a warm home and warm beds in which to stay. We stayed in Johannesburg for two weeks. God opened the door for me to speak in two churches there. We then took a more than six-hour bus ride to Durban, where the pastor from Tongaat and his wife met us at the bus station. They took us to an apartment located near the beach on the Indian Ocean; the name of the town is La Mercy. They prayed with us, and were so happy to receive us. And then they left. It was a beautiful apartment, furnished and stocked with food, etc.

After the pastor and his wife left, we realized that there was no telephone, no means of transportation, and we did not know what would happen next! We had come from our country, where we were constantly busy, constantly ministering to and with the people. And here we found ourselves alone and wondering what was happening. Had we offended the people? We had arrived in the middle of the week, and did not hear anything from anyone until Sunday morning, when the pastor arrived to pick us up for the service! During the service, we shared the story of the attack on our home villages. The people were so touched and grieved by our story that they wept for us and with us. We shared some of the pictures we had taken following the attack, as well as video footage.

Our host pastor made copies of the photos and videos of the attack, and sent those to the headquarters of his denomination. When the pastor made the copies and forwarded them to the headquarters, I had no idea what he intended or what the church leaders might do with them. Then the pastor from Tongaat began trying to organize meetings for us to speak in other churches in the area. He did not have much response from the other churches, though we did have a few invitations to speak. After a few weeks, we were no longer receiving invitations to speak at other churches. So we found ourselves sitting in the apartment in a foreign country with little to do. We began to feel depressed. We even questioned if we had made a big mistake in coming to South Africa. We had tickets for our return to Pakistan, but they were for a date still almost two months away. I told my wife, "We are not going to eat, we are not going to drink, we are not going to sleep on the beds—we are going to sleep on the floor, until God answers our prayers and opens a door for ministry."

We had been fasting and praying for two days, with no food or drink, sleeping on the hard floor—even with our children on the hard floor. There was a knock at the door that evening. When I opened the door, I saw our neighbor (in the next apartment). He told me that he was a Christian, and a police officer. He said that it was his daughter's birthday, and that we were invited to come to the party. We were so happy that someone had reached out to us. We went to the birthday party, and my neighbor introduced us to his pastor. His pastor was very happy to meet us, and promised that he would come the following day to pick us up and take us to the local pastors' meeting. We were praising the Lord for answering our prayer. The next day when we went to the local pastors' meeting, I was given the opportunity to speak. When I spoke, the Spirit of God came down in a mighty way. The word God had given me to speak touched the hearts of these local pastors. Almost all of them then invited me to come and speak in their churches.

Suddenly, we were busy in ministry, just like we had been at home in Pakistan. I was invited to speak three to four times every week. It was a great time of blessing, and God moved so powerfully and blessed many people. As we were ministering and going from church to church, the days passed quickly.

CHAPTER 19

We Cannot Go Home Again

About a week before our visas were to expire, and we were to return to Pakistan, we learned that the copies of the photos and video footage that had been made by the host pastor had impacted the church leaders at the denominational headquarters so much that they joined other pastors in organizing a protest in front of the Pakistani Embassy in Pretoria, South Africa (the nation's capital).

The Christian protesters told the ambassador that the Pakistani government should be treating Christians with respect and fairness. The Christians then threatened to shut down the Pakistani Embassy in Pretoria if their government was unwilling to treat Pakistani Christians with justice and equality. They further threatened to prevent the Pakistani cricket team from participating in the international tournaments in South Africa. Cricket is the national sport of Pakistan. The threat of disallowing the Pakistani team's participation in the international competition was considered a very serious situation. The ambassador responded by denying the facts, insisting that the attack never happened. The Christians accused the ambassador of lying. The ambassador then asked them who had given them the information regarding the attacks. They told him my name, and he then reported me to the government of Pakistan.

My name was then published in newspapers. From that point on, we knew it would be impossible to return to Pakistan. We knew we could not return because we read newspaper articles reporting that the

Prime Minister of Pakistan had called the High Commissioner of the South African Consulate General in Islamabad about the protest. Also, some of our friends in Pakistan informed us that because of the South African protest against the Muslims and the Pakistani government, my name had been added to the government's black list. If we had returned under those circumstances, we would have been arrested at the airport, and then killed or imprisoned for the rest of our lives.

This happened at the end of August 1997. When we learned of the whole situation, we began to realize that we could not return to the land of our births, to our family, to our Christian brothers and sisters with whom we had ministered, and the friends with whom we had grown up—all the people with whom we had shared good times, bad times, times of rejoicing, times of sorrow, times of overcoming, and times of loss. It was a total shock.

We cried, and we cried that day. I cried out to God asking Him to tell me why He allowed this thing to happen. The Lord comforted me with His Word from Matthew 10:37 (KJV): "He that loveth father or mother more than me is not worthy of me: and he that loveth son or daughter more than me is not worthy of me." In His wonderful grace, He also gave me Psalm 27:10 (KJV): "When my father and my mother forsake me, then the LORD will take me up."

When Christians in South Africa found out that we would not be able to return to Pakistan, their attitudes and behavior toward us dramatically changed. It seemed that they saw us as a burden, a burden they no longer wanted to bear. They began to treat us like second-class people, and began to withdraw from us. We realized that not only had we lost our homeland, we were also losing our new family in South Africa. During that time, there was a service in another town, and when we returned to our apartment a few days later, we learned that the family that had allowed us to stay in the apartment had returned to it. They had moved back in, and they had packed our belongings and placed them in a corner. They had even changed the door locks!

We were stunned as we realized our circumstances. We had two little babies (seven months and twenty-two months), but no milk to feed them. We used someone's phone to call the pastor who had first brought us to the apartment. He finally came with the key so that we could get our belongings. He then took us to the home of one of his church members. When we arrived there, we saw that they had a very big home with many rooms. We were so grateful that we would have a nice place to stay. But another great shock was in store for us, when the host family showed us a room. It was a very small room with one queen-sized bed. When we looked at the bed, we could see that the bedsheet was full of dog hair. We could not help but think that they were giving us their dog's bed. We had quickly gone from being in a comfortable apartment to now having one small room, with one bed to be shared by the four of us, a bed that had clearly been used by the dog. Even in our shock and despair, we gave thanks to the Lord because we at least had a roof over our heads.

Then, another shock … our hostess told us that when we washed the baby bottles, we needed to be certain that we limited water use to one glass of water. She further instructed that when we took showers, we were not to splash any water on the shower walls. Although my wife regularly helped our hostess with food preparation and other housekeeping duties, we could clearly sense that our host and hostess were not happy to have us in their home. Anytime that we came out of our room, their dog began to bark at us, and my younger daughter (at that time she was nine months old) would begin to cry because she was afraid of the dog. We believed the dog was barking at us because he was not happy that we had taken his room. Our hostess told my wife, "Tell your daughter that she must understand that the dog is a little baby of ten months old. She must not cry because it upsets the dog!"

CHAPTER 20

Alone in a Foreign Land

What a difficult time for us. We were foreigners in a country not our own. We could not safely return to our homeland. We were challenged by the cultural differences, experienced bigotry because of our skin color, and were dependent on others. We had no money, no telephone, and no car. We were a young, married couple with two children. As a husband and father, I felt a deep responsibility to provide for my family. Every day seemed worse, and I seemed less able to find a way to care for my family. Depression began to take hold, almost like a fog filtering into my mind. At one low point, I contemplated taking our family for a walk into the ocean, continuing to walk until our lives were ended.

One day I was tuning a small shortwave radio. I found a station broadcasting a program called *Grace to You*, by Pastor John MacArthur. The message he shared that morning was surely meant for me! A renewal of hope washed over me, just as though God was speaking directly to me through the radio. As the tears flowed freely, I knew the Lord was delivering me from my depression and suicidal thoughts.

For fourteen months, during much of our time in South Africa, my wife and I listened to Pastor MacArthur's messages. We also discovered Dr. Charles Swindoll broadcasting from the United States, and Pastor Dhinakaran and Pastor Ajit Horo from India. Day after day we listened to these four preachers on our knees. We put the radio on a high shelf. When these men began to preach, we would go to our knees, and tears would begin to roll down our faces. I praise God for these servants of His, who helped us so much through these radio programs.

I could not have imagined then that one day I would be blessed to meet some of these men of God. After coming to the United States, I received a phone call from a Bible college called Master's College. They asked me to speak in their chapel. I did not know until I arrived there that Master's College was founded by John MacArthur. There I was speaking in the chapel of the college founded by one of those preachers I had listened to for those fourteen difficult months in South Africa. I was so greatly blessed and honored to speak there. I thank God for making it possible for me to do so.

We also listened to Pastor Ajit Horo from India. Each day when he preached his message, it was exactly what we needed for that day, and we were greatly encouraged. He preached in Hindi. We were so blessed through his messages. When we were there in South Africa, I also had a desire to meet Pastor Horo, though I never imagined that would be possible.

In July 2009, a Christian singer from India, Balbir Sufi, came to our Pakistani church in Colorado. My wife attended the services. The next day she called me and told me that she sensed in her spirit that we should invite the brother to our home for tea. I agreed, and we arranged a time with him. Another Pakistani brother, Akeel Masih, brought him to our home. We had a wonderful time of fellowship with brother Sufi. He invited me to come to India and be a part of his next recording project. He wanted me to share a five-minute gospel message on his next CD. He is very well-known in India and Pakistan, and records music in Hindi, Punjabi, and Urdu. We agreed to go to India and arranged a time that was agreeable to all of us.

About one week before we were scheduled to leave, I called brother Suffi, and told him that when I was in South Africa, I used to listen to a preacher on the radio named Ajit Horo. I asked him if he could get the contact information of this pastor so that we could try to see him while we were in India. Two or three days later, brother Sufi called me back with the cell phone number for Pastor Horo! I called Pastor Horo and told him who I was and that we had been greatly blessed when we listened to his sermons on FEBA (Far East Broadcast Association) Radio while we were in South Africa. I also told him that I was coming to India and that I would like to meet him if that was possible.

As a Christian preacher, I know that we have ups and downs in ministry. Sometimes our faith is so high, higher than the mountains. And at other times we almost feel like we are drowning! The day I called Pastor Horo, he was feeling very low in the spirit. He told me, "Brother, I am so happy that you called me. Today as you told me that as you listened to my sermons while you were in South Africa, they were a great blessing to you and your wife—your call today is for me just like my sermons were for you."

I praise God. God made it possible for us to meet with Pastor Horo, his wife, and children. We went to their home for a meal. The Lord led me to wash the feet of this man of God. We prayed together and praised the Lord for His wonderful ways.

CHAPTER 21

Moving Out of the Dog's Room

One day while we were living with the family who had given us the "dog's room," I called one of my old friends, Pastor Ravi, that I had met while in Bible college in Pakistan. I explained our situation to him and begged him to come and rescue us! We thank God that he came the following day. We loaded our belongings into his car, and he took us to his home. We stayed in his home for a few days, and then he returned us to our host church in Tongaat. I tried to explain what had happened with the host family from his congregation, but the pastor from Tongaat was angry with us. He told us that we were unappreciative. Despite his anger, he did arrange another home for us. We were so grateful because we felt more welcome in that home. We remained there for two weeks, at which time the pastor told me that as I was preaching in the churches in that area, all of the money which I received from the churches must be given to him. He said he would then rent an apartment for us.

Prior to raising sufficient funds for renting an apartment, I remembered two sisters that we had met while attending Covenant Bible College. They had come to visit us while we were still in Pakistan. I decided to contact them, and, thank God, they welcomed us into their home and arranged some meetings in their churches. Sister Ruckmoney hosted us in her home for several weeks. One week prior to moving into her home, we were attending a church service in Tongaat. While listening to the sermon, the Lord brought Isaiah 58 (KJV) to my mind—specifically the verses relating to fasting:

Cry aloud, spare not, lift up thy voice like a trumpet, and shew my people their transgression, and the house of Jacob their sins. Yet they seek me daily, and delight to know my ways, as a nation that did righteousness, and forsook not the ordinance of their God: they ask of me the ordinances of justice; they take delight in approaching to God. Wherefore have we fasted, say they, and thou seest not? wherefore have we afflicted our soul, and thou takest no knowledge? Behold, in the day of your fast ye find pleasure, and exact all your labours. Behold, ye fast for strife and debate, and to smite with the fist of wickedness: ye shall not fast as ye do this day, to make your voice to be heard on high. Is it such a fast that I have chosen? a day for a man to afflict his soul? is it to bow down his head as a bulrush, and to spread sackcloth and ashes under him? wilt thou call this a fast, and an acceptable day to the LORD? Is not this the fast that I have chosen? to loose the bands of wickedness, to undo the heavy burdens, and to let the oppressed go free, and that ye break every yoke? Is it not to deal thy bread to the hungry, and that thou bring the poor that are cast out to thy house? when thou seest the naked, that thou cover him; and that thou hide not thyself from thine own flesh? Then shall thy light break forth as the morning, and thine health shall spring forth speedily: and thy righteousness shall go before thee; the glory of the LORD shall be thy reward. Then shalt thou call, and the LORD shall answer; thou shalt cry, and he shall say, Here I am. If thou take away from the midst of thee the yoke, the putting forth of the finger, and speaking vanity; And if thou draw out thy soul to the hungry, and satisfy the afflicted soul; then shall thy light rise in obscurity, and thy darkness be as the noon day: And the LORD shall guide thee continually, and satisfy thy soul in drought, and make fat thy bones: and thou shalt be like a watered garden, and like a spring of water, whose waters fail not. And they that shall be of thee shall build the old waste places: thou shalt raise up the foundations of many generations; and thou shalt be called, The repairer of the breach, The restorer of paths to dwell in. If thou turn away thy foot from the sabbath, from doing thy pleasure on my holy day; and call the sabbath a delight, the holy of the LORD, honourable; and shalt honour him, not doing thine own ways, nor finding thine own pleasure, nor speaking thine own words: Then shalt thou delight thyself in the LORD; and I will cause thee to ride upon the high places of the earth, and feed thee with the heritage of Jacob thy father: for the mouth of the LORD hath spoken it.

The Lord inspired me to fast for forty days. I began fasting, sometimes going without food or water for seventy-two hours at a time. When we moved to sister Ruckmoney's home, there was not a lot for us to do much of the time. We prayed for many hours each day. I was still fasting, and I remember one day I felt in my heart that the Lord wanted me to pray for the "healing of kidneys." I spent many hours praying for the healing of kidneys, though I had no idea who had a need for healing of his/her kidneys. After many hours of prayer, I felt peace and felt that He had answered my prayer.

Shortly after we moved in to Sister Ruckmoney's home, the Lord led me to speak to my hostess and tell her that she must reconcile with her daughter-in-law. I told the Lord, "I am not going to do that. We are in such a difficult situation. We have no place to live, no food to eat, no car to drive. She has been very kind toward us. If I tell her what you have told me to, she will kick us out of her home. Then, where will I take my wife and two babies?" But, the Lord kept insisting that I tell her. I kept refusing and reminding Him of our desperate situation.

One evening, our hostess asked me to go with her to a home church meeting. We agreed to go with her. I remember that it was raining cats and dogs that evening. The Lord put in my heart again that I must tell her that she must reconcile with her daughter-in-law. I said, "Lord, you can see that it is raining so hard." I did not tell her! We went into the meeting and had a wonderful service. The people then asked if I would pray for some of the people gathered there.

They brought a couple before me. I had never met this couple. As I laid my hands on their heads, God gave me a word of knowledge. I began telling the man, "You drank alcohol today. You have beaten your wife, and you have threatened her with divorce. You must repent and ask God to forgive you." He was in awe. How could I know all those things? I had never met him before. He realized that it was God speaking to him, telling him that he must repent. He fell to his knees and began to repent. As he did so, he reconciled with his wife—their marriage was restored.

Right then the Lord impressed on my heart that I should now tell my hostess that she must reconcile with her daughter-in-law. In that moment, I was no longer afraid, for the presence of the Lord was so strong. His anointing had been so strong as I ministered to the brother that I was reminded of Elijah and the false prophets.

> Now therefore send, and gather to me all Israel unto mount Carmel, and the prophets of Baal four hundred and fifty, and the prophets of the groves four hundred, which eat at Jezebel's table. So Ahab sent unto all the children of Israel, and gathered the prophets together unto mount Carmel. And Elijah came unto all the people, and said, How long halt ye between two opinions? if the LORD be God, follow him: but if Baal, then follow him. And the people answered him not a word. Then said Elijah unto the people, I, even I only, remain a prophet of the LORD; but Baal's prophets are four hundred and fifty men. Let them therefore give us two bullocks; and let them choose one bullock for themselves, and cut it in pieces, and lay it on wood, and put no fire under: and I will dress the other bullock, and lay it on wood, and put no fire under: And call ye

on the name of your gods, and I will call on the name of the LORD: and the God that answereth by fire, let him be God. And all the people answered and said, It is well spoken. And Elijah said unto the prophets of Baal, Choose you one bullock for yourselves, and dress it first; for ye are many; and call on the name of your gods, but put no fire under. And they took the bullock which was given them, and they dressed it, and called on the name of Baal from morning even until noon, saying, O Baal, hear us. But there was no voice, nor any that answered. And they leaped upon the altar which was made. And it came to pass at noon, that Elijah mocked them, and said, Cry aloud: for he is a god; either he is talking, or he is pursuing, or he is in a journey, or peradventure he sleepeth, and must be awaked. And they cried aloud, and cut themselves after their manner with knives and lancets, till the blood gushed out upon them. And it came to pass, when midday was past, and they prophesied until the time of the offering of the evening sacrifice, that there was neither voice, nor any to answer, nor any that regarded. And Elijah said unto all the people, Come near unto me. And all the people came near unto him. And he repaired the altar of the LORD that was broken down. And Elijah took twelve stones, according to the number of the tribes of the sons of Jacob, unto whom the word of the LORD came, saying, Israel shall be thy name: And with the stones he built an altar in the name of the LORD: and he made a trench about the altar, as great as would contain two measures of seed. And he put the wood in order, and cut the bullock in pieces, and laid him on the wood, and said, Fill four barrels with water, and pour it on the burnt sacrifice, and on the wood. And he said, Do it the second time. And they did it the second time. And he said, Do it the third time. And they did it the third time. And the water ran round about the altar; and he filled the trench also with water. And it came to pass at the time of the offering of the evening sacrifice, that Elijah the prophet came near, and said, LORD God of Abraham, Isaac, and of Israel, let it be known this day that thou art God in Israel, and that I am thy servant, and that I have done all these things at thy word. Hear me, O LORD, hear me, that this people may know that thou art the LORD God, and that thou hast turned their heart back again. Then the fire of the LORD fell, and consumed the burnt sacrifice, and the wood, and the stones, and the dust, and licked up the water that was in the trench. And when all the people saw it, they fell on their faces: and they said, The LORD, he is the God; the LORD, he is the God. And Elijah said unto them, Take the prophets of Baal; let not one of them escape. And they took them: and Elijah brought them down to the brook Kishon, and slew them there. (1 Kings 18:19–40 KJV)

I turned to Sister Ruckmoney and told her that I wanted to pray for her and that I had a message from the Lord for her. I laid my hand on her and said, "This is what the Lord desires for you to do. You must reconcile with your daughter-in-law. You have not spoken with her in several years. You must repent."

She fell to her knees and began to scream, "How many times must I forgive her?" I reminded her of Jesus's words in Matthew 18:21–22 (KJV): "Then came Peter to him, and said, Lord, how oft shall my brother sin against me, and I forgive him? till seven times? Jesus saith unto him, I say not unto thee, Until seven times: but, Until seventy times seven." Then I prayed for her, that the Lord would bless and comfort her, give her peace and empower her to do what He had called her to do.

By this time, the service was almost over. Two of the elders asked me if I would go with them to pray for their cousin, who was Hindu. She was suffering with kidney problems. Both of her own kidneys were no longer functioning, and her brother had donated one of his. But the new kidney was not functioning properly. She had been unable to eat solid foods for twelve years, living on liquids only all that time. Whenever she had attempted to eat any solid food, she would vomit. The doctors had said there was nothing more they could do. In that moment I remembered that the Lord had instructed me to pray for kidneys, though I did not know who I was praying for. I felt this lady was the one.

As we traveled to her home, the elders explained that the brother who had donated the kidney was a Hindu priest (witch doctor) at the temple, as well as having a small temple in his home. As a Hindu priest, he did what witch doctors do, praying to demons and false gods. When we arrived at the home, I prayed for the woman. Jesus healed her! I told her to eat some solid food. When she ate, she did not vomit! She was able to eat and keep it down. She accepted Jesus Christ as her Lord and Savior that night. Praise the Lord! (I learned later that she did not have any problems after that either. God gave her new kidneys!)

After praying for her, I prayed for the demons and devils of Hinduism, the gods and goddesses, to leave in the name of Jesus. As I prayed, her brother, the Hindu priest and kidney donor, jumped right in front of me. Stuttering, he told me that I could not tell the gods to leave the house. I told him that it was too late. I could not change my prayer. What I had prayed, I prayed! When I said that, he ran out of the house and went to his little temple outside of the house. He began to pray to his Hindu gods, pleading with them to send curses on me. Aware of what he was doing, I prayed again, asking the Lord for His protection for us so that we would not be affected by the curses.

Following that visit, we returned to the home where the church meeting had been. On the way there, I began to experience fear again. I was once again afraid of our hostess because of the message I had delivered to her. It was still raining. I was afraid that she was going to be very angry with us and would throw us out. The questions came again. What would I do? Where would I take my family? I shared my concern with the two elders. I asked for their phone numbers so that if something happened when we returned to her home, at least we could call them. They gave me their numbers.

When we got back to the church gathering from the Hindu home, our hostess was ready to return to her home. She didn't say anything to us. She didn't ask us to get into the car for the ride back home. We simply got in. All the way back home, she did not speak to us. She did not say good night as she usually did. We quietly went to our room. I felt like we had committed a crime against her by sharing the message with her. It was such a quiet, and a very sad, night for us. We spent a lot of time in prayer that night. We committed the whole situation into the Lord's hands. We also prayed that God's fear would grip her heart, and that she would not ask us to leave her home.

The next morning came, and our hostess left home for work very quietly, without saying goodbye and without preparing any breakfast for us as she usually did. We continued to pray. About eleven that morning, our hostess returned. She was shouting with joy and calling for me, "Pastor, Pastor. Look what God has done. This morning my daughter-in-law came to my workplace. She brought this doll and a card for me." The doll was holding a card with the word "peace" on it. "She asked me to forgive her. We have been reconciled. Praise the Lord. Last night when you gave me the message from the Lord, I felt so bad. I was so mad at you guys. I am so sorry that I didn't even say good night, or say good morning or prepare your breakfast. Please forgive me. I want to assure you that that message was from the Lord. I was really amazed. Why did my daughter-in-law come and ask for forgiveness? You have not even met her or told her about the situation."

I told her, "God is a miracle-working God. Although I did not talk to her, nor have I ever even met her, the God who gave you the message through me must have spoken directly to her also. I am so pleased to know that you now have peace between you and your daughter-in-law."

The following day, Sunday, I was still fasting. I spoke in their church. Her daughter-in-law approached me and told me that we were all invited to her home following the service. Praise Jesus! After many years, this family was going to be eating together, in love and harmony. That day I broke my fast in their home! What a wonderful celebration it was! Praise the Lord! What a good God we serve!

CHAPTER 22

Dwelling in the Secret Place

There are so many demonic activities in South Africa. A few days after our hostess had reconciled with her daughter-in-law, she said, "Pastor, we need to go and pray for a lady. She is possessed by demons." She didn't give me any details about the lady or her family. We went to the home, and I prayed for the lady. God delivered her right away! She was free! Then they told me that they had another problem. They had been building a house. They would build up the walls with cement blocks, increasing the height of the walls by a few feet. By this time, it was the end of the day. The next morning, when they would go out to begin working again, the walls that had been completed the day before would be knocked down. This pattern had repeated itself many times. The Lord put on my heart to walk around the perimeter of the whole property seven times, and command the demons to be gone in the name of Jesus. Praise God! I later learned that they were able to build a beautiful home and that the lady was completely and totally delivered.

After a few weeks with Sister Ruckmoney, we returned to Tongaat, where the pastor had rented an apartment for us. We were so grateful to move into our own place, even though it was not a safe environment because of high crime rates. There were burglar alarms, and barred windows and doors on most of the apartments, but our apartment had none of those things. Thank God for that! We learned to rely more and more on Jehovah Nissi, our banner, for our protection. Our situation caused us to pray many hours each day, and He was so faithful. We were reminded every day of Psalm 23 and Psalm 91.

"The LORD is my shepherd; I shall not want. He maketh me to lie down in green pastures; He leadeth me beside the still waters. He restoreth my soul; He leadeth me in the paths of righteousness for His name's sake. Yea, though I walk through the valley of the shadow of death, I will fear no evil; for thou are with me; Thy rod and thy staff, they comfort me. Thou preparest a table before me in the presence of my enemies; Thou anointest my head with oil; my cup runneth over. Surely goodness and mercy shall follow me all the days of my life; and I will dwell in the house of the LORD forever" (Psalm 23 KJV).

"He that dwelleth in the secret place of the most High shall abide under the shadow of the Almighty. I will say of the LORD, He is my refuge and my fortress: my God; in him will I trust. Surely he shall deliver thee from the snare of the fowler, and from the noisome pestilence. He shall cover thee with his feathers, and under his wings shalt thou trust: his truth shall be thy shield and buckler. Thou shalt not be afraid for the terror by night; nor for the arrow that flieth by day; Nor for the pestilence that walketh in darkness; nor for the destruction that wasteth at noonday. A thousand shall fall at thy side, and ten thousand at thy right hand; but it shall not come nigh thee. Only with thine eyes shalt thou behold and see the reward of the wicked. Because thou hast made the LORD, which is my refuge, even the most High, thy habitation; There shall no evil befall thee, neither shall any plague come nigh thy dwelling. For he shall give his angels charge over thee, to keep thee in all thy ways. They shall bear thee up in their hands, lest thou dash thy foot against a stone. Thou shalt tread upon the lion and adder: the young lion and the dragon shalt thou trample under feet. Because he hath set his love upon me, therefore will I deliver him: I will set him on high, because he hath known my name. He shall call upon me, and I will answer him: I will be with him in trouble; I will deliver him, and honour him. With long life will I satisfy him, and shew him my salvation" (Psalm 91 KJV).

While we were living at the apartment, we met a lady one day. She was a Muslim and appeared to be poor. She said she was interested in learning about Jesus Christ. She came to our apartment. We told her about Jesus. She said she would go to church. She mentioned some of her financial needs. We did help her and also asked the church we were attending to help her. After receiving some help from us, she went to the church office and got some money there. After the following Sunday, I called the pastor and asked him if she had been at the service, since she had promised to go. He told me that she had not come. I was surprised that she had lied to us. I was not happy that she had lied about going to church and that she had acted poor just to get money from us and the church.

We have learned that sometimes witches and warlocks will pretend to be people in need, and will approach churches presenting themselves as poor, destitute, and needy—only to infiltrate the church.

A few days later, while I was standing outside of our apartment on the balcony, I saw the same lady coming toward our apartment. She was carrying a kitten. My wife and I had both studied demonology and witchcraft with the Christian perspective on how to defeat the Devil and his demons. When I told my wife that the lady was coming our way, carrying a kitten, my wife said, "Tell her she is welcome to come into our apartment, but she cannot bring the kitten in." We knew that the witches and warlocks use cats and kittens to cast spells. So I told the lady, "You are welcome to come into our house, but you must leave the kitten outside." So she left the kitten outside in the basket and came inside. We gave her some food and some money, and I asked her why she had not gone to church. She gave me an unsatisfactory excuse, and I sensed in my spirit that she was not really sincere. There was something more going on under the surface. So, after she was gone, I prayed to God: "God, please reveal to me who this lady is. Is she really sincere when she says she wants to know You? Who is she?"

My wife and I prayed about her when we went to sleep that night. About two in the morning, I had a dream. In that dream I saw what appeared to be the claw of a wolf coming to attack my younger daughter, who was sleeping right next to me. The Holy Spirit awakened me. I prayed, and the claw disappeared. I was impressed to open the curtain on the window beside my bed and see what was happening outside. I was very shocked. The lady, the same one who had brought the kitten, was outside right under the window, looking up and spewing curses toward us. The Spirit of the Lord came upon me in a very powerful way at that very moment. I prayed and commanded those curses not to fall on us. I saw a ball of fire, like lightning, go out the window. It was like two powerful forces fighting. I knew that fire comes from God. When the fire fell on her, the lady took off. She ran. Praise God! Through the power of the Holy Spirit, we were able to overcome the power of the devil. We found out that the lady was a witch. A few days later, I saw her again. I could see that she had a large burn on her leg! You cannot play with the fire of God!

It is helpful to understand that Muslims believe that there are good demons and bad demons. The good demons are called *jinns*. One time Mohammed was reciting the Qur'an, and some demons (*jinns*) came to him and told him that they really liked his recitation of the Qur'an. Mohammed took that opportunity to invite the demons to become Muslim, and so they did! Also, in the Qur'an, Allah has appointed some angels to cause division between husbands and wives. Growing up in Pakistan, we were taught that in order to achieve your goals and desires or to send curses on people, you needed to chant certain Suras from the Qur'an at certain times of the day for a specific number of repetitions.

Let me give you an explanation of witches and witch doctors. For many people, especially raised in Western cultures, witches are believed to be only part of witchcraft. Too often they are dismissed as fantasy and promoted as Halloween fun. An understanding of witch doctors is similar. They are only part of tribal societies in the jungles of Africa. Understanding the reality of witches and witch doctors is decreased also by the lack of understanding of the reality of satanic forces at work in the world.

Witchcraft certainly does exist, as do witches and warlocks. Witch doctors do exist and do still apply their incantations, spells, and potions. One of the key "tools of the trade" in the occult is the sending of curses. The dictionary defines curse as: (1) the expression of a wish that misfortune, evil, doom, etc., befall a person, group, etc.; (2) a formula or charm intended to cause such misfortune to another.

While we may have some understanding that pronouncing a curse is evil, intended to bring harm or bad things into someone else's life, I believe there is another aspect of cursing someone else. Consider that when a parent says to a child, "You are not smart enough to take that class." Or, "You cannot have piano lessons because you have no musical talent." Or, "Don't even think about trying out for the team because you are just not athletic." Or worse, "You will never amount to anything." What about when a husband tells his wife, "You just can't cook like my momma." Or, "You have no right to help decide what we do with the money in this house. I'm the one with the job so I will decide." What about when a wife tells her husband, "Why can't you be more like my dad?" Or, "When are you going to get a real job so you can take better care of me?"

I think you understand the point I am trying to make with these statements. These are not words that are life-giving. They do not speak encouragement, affirmation, or acceptance. When you consider that the opposite of life is death, we can begin to realize that these can become words of death. While they may not lead to physical death, they can—especially when repeated often over time—kill a person's hopes and dreams and rob whatever belief he/she might have had in himself/herself. Words of death heard again and again over time can also affect someone's belief in God or understanding of His true character. Beyond that, by speaking those kinds of things, we are actually inviting the demonic and evil forces to come against them, encouraging them to do and become what we have already accused them of doing or who we have accused them of being.

Let's look at what the Word of God says about our tongues:

Proverbs 18:20–21 (KJV) says this: "A man's belly shall be satisfied with the fruit of his mouth; and with the increase of his lips shall he be filled. Death and life are in the power of the tongue: and they that love it shall eat the fruit thereof."

> For in many things we offend all. If any man offend
> not in word, the same is a perfect man, and able also to
> bridle the whole body. Behold, we put bits in the horses'

mouths, that they may obey us; and we turn about their whole body. Behold also the ships, which though they be so great, and are driven of fierce winds, yet are they turned about with a very small helm, whithersoever the governor listeth. Even so the tongue is a little member, and boasteth great things. Behold, how great a matter a little fire kindleth! And the tongue is a fire, a world of iniquity: so is the tongue among our members, that it defileth the whole body, and setteth on fire the course of nature; and it is set on fire of hell. For every kind of beasts, and of birds, and of serpents, and of things in the sea, is tamed, and hath been tamed of mankind: But the tongue can no man tame; it is an unruly evil, full of deadly poison. Therewith bless we God, even the Father; and therewith curse we men, which are made after the similitude of God. Out of the same mouth proceedeth blessing and cursing. My brethren, these things ought not so to be. Doth a fountain send forth at the same place sweet water and bitter? Can the fig tree, my brethren, bear olive berries? either a vine, figs? so can no fountain both yield salt water and fresh. (James 3:2–12 (KJV)

And here is what the Word of God says about what we are to do with our tongues:

"Let them curse, but bless thou: when they arise, let them be ashamed; but let thy servant rejoice" (Psalm 109:28 KJV).

"But I say unto you which hear, Love your enemies, do good to them which hate you, Bless them that curse you, and pray for them which despitefully use you" (Luke 6:27–28 KJV).

"Bless them which persecute you: bless, and curse not" (Romans 12:14 KJV).

The Lord makes it very clear throughout His Word that we are to speak blessings, not curses. We are to speak life, not death. In the previous verses, God is really commanding us to bless those who persecute us, and to bless those who curse us. The only shield we have against those curses which are sent toward us from others is the blessing we speak over their lives. When we bless those who are cursing us, it is protecting us. It is protecting me, my family, ministry, and everything which God has given to me. Plus, it not only protects us, but the prayer we have prayed for those who curse us is going to come back on us. You might be wondering what I mean by that. In Luke 10:5–6 (KJV) we read the words of Jesus: "And into whatsoever house ye enter, first say, Peace be to this house. And if the son of peace be there, your peace shall rest upon it: if not, it shall turn to you again." Do you see the dual shield against the curses and intended destruction?

It is also vital that we recognize that when we continue to speak curses, tearing someone down rather than building them up, we are rebelling against God. When we read in 1 Samuel 15, we discover what His Word says about rebellion:

> And Samuel said, "When thou wast little in thine own sight, wast thou not made the head of the tribes of Israel, and the LORD anointed thee king over Israel? And the LORD sent thee on a journey, and said, Go and utterly destroy the sinners the Amalekites, and fight against them until they be consumed. Wherefore then didst thou not obey the voice of the LORD, but didst fly upon the spoil, and didst evil in the sight of the LORD? And Saul said unto Samuel, Yea, I have obeyed the voice of the LORD, and have gone the way which the LORD sent me, and have brought Agag the king of Amalek, and have utterly destroyed the Amalekites. But the people took of the spoil, sheep and oxen, the chief of the things which should have been utterly destroyed, to sacrifice unto the LORD thy God in Gilgal. And Samuel said, Hath the LORD as great delight in burnt offerings and sacrifices, as in obeying the voice of the LORD? Behold, to obey is better than sacrifice, and to hearken than the fat of rams. **For rebellion is as the sin of witchcraft,**

and stubbornness is as iniquity and idolatry. Because thou hast rejected the word of the LORD, he hath also rejected thee from being king." (1 Samuel 15:17–23 KJV, emphasis mine)

I challenge you to ask yourself this question: When someone spoke negatively about you, or cursed you, what was your response? Did you get angry? Did you speak negatively about them? If you spoke angrily or negatively, it would be as though you removed your "bulletproof jacket"—allowing his/her curses and negativity to be activated in your life. But if you blessed the person, instead of cursing him or her, those curses they aimed at you will actually return to the sender, the one who spoke the curse over you. When we curse those who have cursed us, we are acting as a witch or a witch doctor. How many times have you acted like a witch or witch doctor toward your children, your spouse, your parents, your neighbors, your city, the leader of your country, and even yourself? *Please stop!*

CHAPTER 23

Testimonies Open Doors

One day a couple came to our apartment. We never learned how they had heard about us. When this couple came to us, the Spirit of the Lord came upon me in a mighty way, and I began to tell her the story of the Samaritan woman at the well in John 4. I told her that I sensed her situation was like that of the Samaritan woman. She began to cry and told me, "It is correct. I already had five husbands, and this man with whom I have come is not my husband even though I am living with him." I told her to repent of her sins because Jesus loves her. Thank God, she repented of her sins that day. The man with whom she had come left her there with us.

The woman then began to spread the news that she had met a man, just like Jesus, who had told her about her sins. Because of her testimony, two missionary ladies came to see us the following week. When these two ladies came to our apartment, one fell on the ground and the other said, "There is such a presence of God in this home. We cannot even stand." They told us that we must go immediately with them to their town to preach in their churches. One of the ladies was a pastor's wife, and the other was married to a medical doctor. They took us to their town, and the pastor's wife hosted us in her home. We were welcomed and treated so well. They asked me to preach in their church that Sunday. God moved in a mighty way that day. Many people were blessed and healed. The news about that service began to spread throughout the community. We returned to our apartment after one week in their town.

Though we did not have a telephone in our apartment, I used our landlord's number as a contact number if people wanted to reach us. One day, my landlady came and told me that a woman was on the phone and wanted to talk to me. I went into the landlady's apartment and talked with the woman on the phone. She told me that she had heard about the meeting in Pietermaritzburg, South Africa, the previous week. She was sorry she had been unable to attend the church service. She told me, "I am a Muslim. My mother has breast cancer. I heard that God healed many people through you in the meeting last week. Would you consider praying for my mother, that God might also heal my mother from breast cancer?"

I told her, "Sure I will pray for your mother to be healed from breast cancer. I will even fast for her. But let me clarify here—I am not a healer. Jesus Christ is the healer. He is the only one who can heal your mother." Then, I told her about Jesus, and asked her to pray in the name of Jesus in the future. She promised that she would pray in the name of Jesus. I fasted and prayed for more than two days. Later that week, we learned that the lady with breast cancer had been healed. Glory to Jesus!

The healing miracle was wonderful. But the enemy used the situation to create a problem for us! The lady who was healed had five children. Her four daughters were praising Jesus when their mother was healed. However, her son was not pleased. He was happy that his mother had been healed but was not happy when he learned that his mother had been healed in the name of Jesus. He was a Muslim imam (priest). So, this Muslim imam considered us to be a source of contention in his family. He threatened that they (the imam and other Muslims) were going to come and kill us.

We left the apartment as soon as we learned of the threat. We went to the medical doctor's home in Richmond, South Africa. The name of the medical doctor is Dr. Collin (his wife had been one of the two missionaries who had visited us earlier). They welcomed us into their home, but he did share one requirement with me. He asked that I preach in his medical clinic every morning before he would see the patients.

He also asked that I travel with him to the small villages where he took medicines and saw patients. He wanted me to preach and pray in those villages also.

It was a wonderful offer and opportunity. I was very happy as I began to travel to the small towns and villages, sharing the Word of God and preaching in the doctor's medical clinic. People began giving their lives to Jesus. Many of the people had been involved in witchcraft. They accepted Jesus Christ as their Lord and Savior. They also destroyed all the occult-related objects, including the books, bones, potions, idols, and any familiar objects. It reminded me of Acts 19:18–20 (KJV): "And many that believed came, and confessed, and shewed their deeds. Many of them also which used curious arts brought their books together, and burned them before all men: and they counted the price of them, and found it fifty thousand pieces of silver. So mightily grew the word of God and prevailed." Praise the Lord! The God of the Book of Acts is the same yesterday, today and forever!

One time we went to a village where we were told there was a very famous witch doctor, and that everyone was afraid of him. When I learned about this, I was very excited to see this witch doctor. In those days, I did not have much to do except to fast and pray because of our situation. I remember we sometimes would pray for ten hours in a day. When I went to that village, as soon as I got out of the jeep, I met this witch doctor. He was coming toward us. As he approached me, I said in a loud voice, "In the Name of Jesus Christ of Nazareth, I command you to kneel down." And he knelt down right there. And the Spirit of God was very strongly upon me, and I said to him, "Accept Jesus Christ to be your personal savior right now. Say this prayer after me ..." He said the prayer and accepted Jesus right there. We then went to his home and destroyed all the bones, potions, and demonic things that he used. We then took him to the doctor's home and baptized him in the swimming pool.

As I was preaching at Dr. Collin's clinic, the Muslims in the area learned that I was in the town. There is a big Islamic organization in South Africa, and they assigned some Muslims to find me and kill me. One morning when I went to a store, two Muslim men followed me.

They caught me outside of the store. They were very angry, and told me that I must convert back to Islam. They told me that there is no way that I could be a Christian because I was born in a Muslim country.

According to the Islamic law (Sharia law), Allah is the owner of the entire earth. Allah owns everything, and every child who is born into this world is a Muslim. And, especially because I was born in a Muslim country, there was no way that I could be Christian. They insisted that I must be a Muslim and that I must go with them to the mosque immediately and embrace Islam. "We will take you to the mosque and will talk with you." But, their anger was very intense, and they insisted that I go with them immediately. I tried to explain to them that I had just purchased a loaf of bread and needed to take it back to my wife and children before going to the mosque with them. "I am not afraid to go with you to the mosque, but I must take this bread to my family first."

Thank God, they allowed me to do that. When I arrived at the home, I told our host family what had happened. Dr. Collin then shared that these men had come to his clinic the previous week looking for me and had been very angry. "They may kill you if you go with them. So you had better not go to meet with them." I agreed with the doctor, and did not go back to meet them. Once again it was time for our family to move. Dr. Collin arranged through his church for us to be moved to Johannesburg, South Africa. I was reminded again of a passage from the Word of God: "But Saul increased the more in strength, and confounded the Jews which dwelt at Damascus, proving that this is very Christ. And after that many days were fulfilled, the Jews took counsel to kill him: But their laying await was known of Saul. And they watched the gates day and night to kill him. Then the disciples took him by night, and let him down by the wall in a basket" (Acts 9:22–25 KJV).

CHAPTER 24

Another Move

It was the threat of danger that prompted us to move to Johannesburg. But there were also other reasons for us to make that move. When we realized that we were unable to return to Pakistan, we applied for an extension on our visas. We were given a three-month extension, but we were told that it was the final extension we would be given. The South African government told us that they could not extend our visas any further than that. Some people suggested that we apply for asylum in South Africa. For that purpose, we would have to be renewing our extension every month, and so would need to go to the office in Pretoria each month. Because Johannesburg was near Pretoria, it would be much better for us to live there.

Thank God once again for his provision. The church opened a door for us to be hosted by a widow in Johannesburg, whose name is Julie. The church helped our hostess by reimbursing her for the expenses associated with hosting our family. We thank God for sister Julie and her church. We were so grateful to Him for providing a safe place to live. Her home was completely equipped with a security system.

When we arrived at her home, we felt in our spirits that although the home was equipped with the security system, including the barred windows and doors, protecting it from thieves, we sensed that it was not protected from the devil. We began praying the very day we arrived at her home. I heard a very loud, explosive sound coming from the ceiling. I also heard scratching sounds, like animals clawing. As I prayed, the sounds disappeared. Sister Julie later told me that her computer table had almost tipped over and the monitor had almost fallen. She described it as though there had been an earthquake.

We thanked God that the demonic presence which had caused the sounds left that home. However, we began looking around her home, sensing that there was still something going on in the home. We found some occult-related objects, pornographic magazines, and sexually explicit novels. We told our hostess that they were familiar objects which open the door to demonic activity and that they needed to be removed. She told us that they did not belong to her, but to her late husband, who had brought them from Germany. There were also several decorative pieces relating to Hitler and his Nazi regime. She had kept them because of her late husband's memory and because they had been expensive. But as we explained that these things draw demons into her home, she agreed with us. My wife and I took a hammer and broke all the objects into pieces, and burned the books and magazines.

After we had been staying with her for some time, we still were not totally satisfied that the housecleaning was complete. We felt there was still something that needed to be removed from the home. One day as I prayed, I opened a cupboard, and I saw a number of bottles of liquor. I told Sister Julie that as Christians, we are the temple of the Holy Spirit. We must not allow liquor to defile us. She agreed and was willing to return the liquor to the store. After that, we felt that the house was really clean. We praised the Lord.

God began using us to help other people and their needs for prayer. One day a woman came and asked if I could pray for her friend who was from Turkey. Her friend was in the rug business and was a Muslim. He had married a South African white woman. She explained what was going on with this man in his own home. She told me that the man had told her that the rugs were flying in his home and that demons were coming out of a mirror. He was so afraid of the things that were happening in his home. He tried to stop all of the activities by placing a charm (very well known in Turkey) called an evil eye. He placed evil eyes in his workplace, in his car, and in almost every room in his home, but it was not helping. There was still demonic activity going on. The

Christian lady who had come to me further explained that she had gone to many different churches to ask pastors to come and pray for this man. They responded with a variety of excuses why they could not come.

She learned about me and came to see me to ask if I would go to the man. I told her that I would come, but not immediately. Instead I would go the following week after I had fasted and prayed. The Holy Spirit reminded me of Mark 9:29 (KJV) when Jesus responded as His disciples asked Him why they had been unable to cast out a demon in the deaf mute boy: "And he said unto them, This kind can come forth by nothing, but by prayer and fasting." I told the sister that I needed to fast and pray before going to cast out the demons.

I fasted and prayed for a few days. One day as I prayed, I had a vision. In the vision, two big black dogs ran toward me to attack me, but I got up and attacked and killed the two dogs. As I continued praying, I had a second vision right after the first one. I saw a huge dragon or snake come to me. It wanted to attack me, but the Holy Spirit helped me to kill that dragon. When I killed the dragon in the vision, I picked it up and threw it in the valley. In the vision, I felt like I was standing on top of the mountain. I then knew that I had the victory over the devil. I also knew that I had received the deliverance for that man. I always believe that before I go to pray with someone for deliverance or healing, I need to be on my knees, in my closet, to receive that person's healing or deliverance before I go to pray with them. Thank God!

I called the lady and told her that I was ready to go and pray for the man. An elder from the church went with me to the man's home. We went into his home and prayed. Praise the Lord. The man and his house were delivered from the demonic activity. But then we needed to clean his house. We removed all the evil eyes from the rooms of his home and his car. We told him that the evil eyes could not provide protection. We told him that only Jesus could protect him from evil. Thank God he was willing to give up the objects, even though they were made of gold. We told him that we were going to burn them, because they were not from God. We prayed for him, and he was delivered. We prayed in each room. He told us that he felt different, and there was no longer any demonic presence in his home.

We then invited him to accept the Lord Jesus Christ. When we asked this Muslim man to become a Christian, he was very afraid. He told us that if he became a Christian, his parents, family, and friends would kill him. When he responded like that, we knew that he was controlled by the spirit of fear. We looked right into his eyes, which are the doorways to the man's soul. We commanded the spirit of fear to leave this man in the name of Jesus Christ, so that he could be free. Praise the Lord!

We then repeated the same question, "Would you accept the Lord Jesus Christ? Would you like to become a Christian?" This time he said yes. We then led him in a prayer to accept Jesus Christ as his Lord and Savior. We left his home and burned all the evil eyes and other objects because we remembered Deuteronomy 7:4–6 (KJV): "For they will turn away thy son from following me, that they may serve other gods: so will the anger of the LORD be kindled against you, and destroy thee suddenly. But thus shall ye deal with them; ye shall destroy their altars, and break down their images, and cut down their groves, and burn their graven images with fire. For thou art a holy people unto the LORD thy God: the LORD thy God hath chosen thee to be a special people unto himself, above all people that are upon the face of the earth."

CHAPTER 25

Inspired by Hezekiah

As God was using us in South Africa, I received a letter one day from one of the church elders in Pakistan. He requested that we send some money so that they could build a church building. The church was growing, and there was no longer enough room in the elder's home. They wanted me to send money for a church building. As I have already shared, Christians in Pakistan are very poor. When someone from the Christian community goes abroad, people in Pakistan think that the person must then be rich, and so should be sending money back to the people at home.

I confess that when I received the letter, I was very angry. I thought to myself, "These people have no idea how we have been living. We have been suffering here, running from one place to the next for the safety of our lives." But, in the next moment I felt that God was saying that I was not the one who was going to provide the money to build the church building. God is the One who is going to provide the money for the building.

In those days, I had been reading the story of Hezekiah, how he had received a letter from the Assyrian king:

> And Hezekiah received the letter of the hand of the messengers, and read it: and Hezekiah went up into the house of the LORD, and spread it before the LORD. And Hezekiah prayed before the LORD, and said, O LORD

God of Israel, which dwellest between the cherubims, thou art the God, even thou alone, of all the kingdoms of the earth; thou hast made heaven and earth. LORD, bow down thine ear, and hear: open, LORD, thine eyes, and see: and hear the words of Sennacherib, which hath sent him to reproach the living God. Of a truth, LORD, the kings of Assyria have destroyed the nations and their lands, And have cast their gods into the fire: for they were no gods, but the work of men's hands, wood and stone: therefore they have destroyed them. Now therefore, O LORD our God, I beseech thee, save thou us out of his hand, that all the kingdoms of the earth may know that thou art the LORD God, even thou only. (2 Kings 19:14–19 KJV)

As I thought about Hezekiah, I felt in my heart that I should do the same with the letter I had received from the elder in Pakistan. I prayed over the letter and soaked the letter with my tears. "God, I am not able to provide even one cent for this building. But, you can oh Lord. You can meet all their needs." Two days after my prayer, I received a phone call. Someone in another town wanted to meet me two days later. I went to meet the man, though I did not know why he wanted to meet with me. The only thing that I did know was that he was a Christian brother.

When I met him, he told me that I must bring my family the following week on Thursday for supper. He also asked me to meet him at the same place as our first meeting, and then together we would go on to his home. The following Thursday came, and my wife and I, together with another pastor, went to see this man. When we arrived at his workplace, he offered to take me, my wife, and children in his car to his home.

While we were riding in the car, driving toward his home, all of sudden he asked me this question: "How much money do you need to build a church building in Pakistan?"

I answered, "From 50,000 to 70,000 rand."

He told me, "I will give 50,000 rand tomorrow, to build a church building in Pakistan." I was shocked! I had not mentioned anything about praying for the provision of money to build a church building in Pakistan. I even thought he might be joking. We had a wonderful supper in his home, and then returned to our apartment. The next morning he called us and asked for the information about the church bank account. We gave him the account information. He followed through with what he said he would do, and deposited 50,000 rand into the church account. Praise the Lord!

After six months, he asked me about the progress on the church building in Pakistan. I told him that the church was in the process of being built, but, unfortunately, the people in Pakistan, instead of building one church building, decided it was better to build two churches in two different locations. I further told him that I was afraid that there would not be enough money to complete both of the church buildings. He said, "Pastor, do not worry about the money. I will give you another 50,000 rand." He soon gave us another 50,000 rand. Overall, this man gave us a total of 225,000 rand (approximately $32,142), which allowed us not only to complete both church buildings, but also to build the facility for the Bible College. We praise Jesus!

One time a team was going to Pakistan to minister in our churches. I decided to send 50,000 rand with this team. I went to the bank to withdraw the money to send with the team. Someone found out that I was carrying 50,000 rand in my briefcase. This Christian Brother was aware of our situation. He knew that we were living in a very poor and difficult situation, and he suggested to me that I just send 25,000 to Pakistan for the church building, and keep the other 25,000 to help meet our needs. It was a very sympathetic and caring idea, but it was totally against my conscience. I told him that it would be better for me to die than to use a penny of the money that had been given for the church buildings.

I thank God that He did help me to be a good steward of His money. Many times we say that we trust in God. It is very easy to say that we trust in God because He is worthy to be trusted. There is no dishonesty, sin, or darkness in God. Yes, we can trust in God, but the question is, can God trust us? In other words, are we worthy of

God's trust? I praise Jesus. With His grace and with His help, I can say confidently, with great fear and trembling, "Yes, God does trust me."

As you read this book, I encourage you to spend time with the Lord in prayer and in His Word. Pray that He will be able to talk about us as He spoke of Job before the devil. God was extremely pleased with Job! We are extremely blessed of our God because He is the great God. Are our lives reflecting Him in such a way as to stir His delight in us?

CHAPTER 26

Testing Leads to Testimony

There are nine provinces in South Africa. During the first ten months of our time in South Africa, we stayed in the province of KwaZulu-Natal. Except for the Eastern and Western Cape provinces, we spent the next fourteen months living in the other six provinces. Try to imagine living in six different states in the United States during two years! It was very difficult, especially for my wife and two little babies. We moved from place to place, province to province.

After one year in South Africa we learned that the government was hesitant to allow us to stay. We applied for asylum. Our papers were stolen three times from the Home Affairs Office by Muslims who were working there. We were told to reapply each time. At the same time, our Pakistani passports were about to expire. We continued to apply for almost a year, but never received an answer. At one point, the South African government gave us fifteen days to leave the country and return to Pakistan.

During our second year in South Africa, we also tried to apply for visas to the United States. We went to the Consulate General of the United States, but they refused to give us the visas. They explained the reasons for the denial:

1. We were Pakistani citizens with Pakistani passports, so we needed to return to our own country to apply for US visas at the US Embassy in Pakistan.

2. Because we were applying for a visa from South Africa, we needed to be South African citizens with South African passports.
3. We needed to own property in South Africa.
4. We needed to have a substantial bank account in a South African bank.
5. We needed to have permanent jobs in South Africa.
6. We needed to have a clearance letter from the South African police.

We had none of these! We could not meet any of the requirements for obtaining US visas.

Sometime later, two men came to work in sister Julie's home. She asked me to oversee the construction work they were doing. As we began to talk, these men told me that they knew someone in the government who could help us to get South African passports "under the table." I was double-minded as I contemplated their suggestion. Should I pursue getting the South African passports or not? I even thought, "It may be that God has brought these people to us to provide a way of escape."

I talked with some Christian friends and pastors about the offer to get the South African passports illegally. Some of them suggested that there was nothing wrong with following through with it. Others told me that it would be wrong. Then, my wife and I prayed, and God showed us that if we were to get the South African passports illegally, we could get the US visas without any problem, but there would be no testimony. So, God showed us that we should not follow through with the tempting offer, and to simply wait for His provision. We realized that there is no testimony without a test!

CHAPTER 27

Closing In

The days and months were passing, and things were getting worse and worse. Even the church people in that part of the country began to stay away from us. Sometimes, even our host, Sister Julie seemed to regret that she had opened her home to us. We could read her mind by looking at her face. She was sometimes clearly very upset with us and impatient with our little children. But we continued to pray, "God, have mercy on us. Please comfort Sister Julie, calm her spirit so she will not ask us to leave her home. And, please, God, cause the church to continue to provide reimbursement to Sister Julie for the expenses of having us in her home."

In the beginning of 1999, Sister Julie's attitude toward us really began to change. Every day it was worse, and continued to get worse. We continued to cry out to God to calm her down. Thank God, He did keep her calm. During the month of April of that year, in the middle of the month, about 2:00 a.m. one day, my family was all sleeping. I heard a very loud and clear voice saying, "I am taking you to America." I woke up. I saw that my wife was sleeping, and that my children were sleeping also. I felt in my spirit that this could be the voice of God.

We tried our best to convince the American consulate that they should give us visas because we could not return to Pakistan. We even took some very well-known and respected men with us to the US Consulate so that they could speak on our behalf. We went at least three times to approach the people at the consulate, hoping they would understand our situation and grant us the visas. The more often we went, the angrier they became toward us. They finally told us not to return again, and that we could not have visas even if we had a letter from President Clinton. They told us it was against the law and that there was nothing they could do because their constitution did not allow for granting a visa in South Africa on a Pakistani passport.

My father-in-law was living in the United States at that time. We asked if he could help us to obtain visas for the United States. He hired an immigration attorney to apply for an R1 visa (religious visa). The application was turned down. Then we asked my father-in-law if he could send us a letter from a government official. He did send us a letter from a congresswoman. We took the letter to the US Consulate. They angrily reminded us that they had already told us that even if we had a letter from the president of the United States, we would not be granted a visa. We began to think that we would soon be deported back to Pakistan as the South African government had threatened. We left so discouraged that day. But the Lord inspired me to pray, "God, grant me the favor of this man, even though he has told us we will not receive a visa. If he will not give us the visa, then I ask that you remove him from this position." Thank God! When we later returned to the consulate, that man had been reassigned back to the United States!

During this time, I told my wife that I was ready to die for Jesus. And she told me that she was ready to die for Him as well. But our greatest concern was what would happen to our children. If we were deported to Pakistan, we would immediately be arrested. We realized that government officials might try to break our commitment to Jesus by using our children. A thought came into both of our minds. If someone in South Africa adopted the children, they would be able to live. We were even willing to give up our children so that they could live. We did not know what would happen to us.

We were reminded of the two mothers brought before King Solomon. The real mother of the living child was willing to give up her son, so that he could live.

"And the king said, Divide the living child in two, and give half to the one, and half to the other. Then spake the woman whose the living child was unto the king, for her bowels yearned upon her son, and she said, O my lord, give her the living child, and in no wise slay it. But the other said, Let it be neither mine nor thine, but divide it. Then the king answered and said, Give her the living child, and in no wise slay it: she is the mother thereof" (1 Kings 3:25–27 KJV).

We felt like we were in the same kind of situation. Try to put yourself in our shoes. Think of how difficult it would be to consider giving up your children when you are able to take care of them, but, for their safety, they must be placed with adoptive parents. That is true parental love. God Almighty actually gave up His Son, in order to save the rest of His children. We thank Him for that great sacrifice.

As we were thinking about the possibility of adoption for our children, realizing that we had only fifteen more days before deportation, God inspired my wife to fast again, the way Esther fasted and prayed in the Bible—three days and three nights with no food or water, an absolute fast. As she fasted, we prayed, reminding the Lord of the stories we had heard of how people had smuggled Bibles into restricted nations, how they were searched by the customs agents or police when they arrived in those nations and how they could not even see the Bibles that were being carried by the Christians.

We cried out to God, reminding Him that though we wanted to go to the United States, the US officials would not give us visas. We cried out to Him, reminding Him again of the stories of how He closed the eyes of officials at the borders of nations, extending favor to His children. We invited Him to go with us to the US Consulate, and pleaded with Him to close the eyes of the officials there, so that they would not even be able to see our passports as Pakistani passports, nor the expiration dates on them, nor the stamps that had been placed on our passports by the South African authorities. We prayed and asked the Lord to pay for our visa fee and plane tickets. We also went before Him with the problem of no money to purchase plane tickets, even if we were granted visas. We put it all before Him.

Years before, while we were still in Pakistan, we had read a book called *Tortured for Christ*, written by Richard Wurmbrand, founder of Voice of the Martyrs. I was also blessed to meet Brother Andrew with Open

Door Ministries and hear him speak while still in Pakistan. What both of these men shared about God's protection and provision was powerful. I thank God for bringing their testimonies to our remembrance as we anticipated our next US Consulate visit. And we thank Him for these great men of faith, who by their examples challenged and encouraged us to stand strong in our faith.

As we arrived at the United States consulate in our last attempt to be granted visas, I put out my hand and said, "Lord Jesus, please go with us." We felt such a strong presence of the Lord Jesus Christ. I was holding His hand and walking with Him. As we went inside, we approached the window where we needed to submit the applications. A lady who was a visa officer took our applications. She did not even look up at us, but simply instructed us to come back in three days to collect our passports. She also handed us the receipt for payment for four visa fees. I was amazed and in awe because we had not paid any visa fees. Yet she was handing me the receipt for the visa fees.

To this day, we do not know how those visa fees were paid. But I do believe that God has many angels throughout the earth helping His children in their times of need. If he can blind the eyes of officials so that they cannot see Bibles being smuggled into their nations, He can send an angel to pay visa fees for His Pakistani children trying to get from South Africa to the United States! Just as Jesus instructed Peter to go to the lake, open the mouth of the first fish he caught, and there find a coin to pay their taxes, He is able to provide whatever we need because our God owns everything! Glory to Jesus!

CHAPTER 28

God's Amazing Favor

When we left the US Consulate, the man who had driven us there asked if we were going to the United States. We told him that we were. He asked if we had money for the plane tickets. We told him that we did not. He told us that we should have "big bucks" to be able to buy four plane tickets. It was the month of July, when tickets were very expensive. We told him that we did not have big bucks, but that we serve a big God! From the time that I gave my life to Jesus, He has instructed me to live by faith. So, we have lived by faith and continue to live by faith here in our new country. He is our provider, our portion, and our Lord! His Word tells us that He will never leave us or forsake us, so we can trust Him to meet us at the point of every one of our needs.

On July 4, 1999, I was sitting in the church in South Africa with my wife and children. There was a time of praise and testimonies. One couple went to the front and shared that they were moving to the United States the following week. That very moment, the Lord spoke to my heart, "You should not come to church next Sunday (July 11), but fast and pray. Then, come back to church on the eighteenth of July, and you will share just like the couple that shared that they are going to the United States." When we heard the testimony of this couple, we had not even returned to the consulate, nor did we even know if we would or could. We applied for our visas for the United States on July 8, and we were told to come back after three business days.

As we waited to return to the consulate, believing we would pick up our visas and passports, the Lord instructed me to get up at 4:00 a.m. on Monday morning, July 12. He further instructed me to do spiritual warfare against the spirit of Pharaoh. Interestingly, as the Israelites were in Egypt, on the continent of Africa, so were we on the continent of Africa in South Africa. As Pharaoh was not allowing the Israelites to leave Egypt for their promised land, the devil was creating problems, hindering us from getting to our promised land. I began to pray. My wife soon joined me, and we continued praying and crying before God. As we were praying, through our tears, people from the church, who had arranged for us to stay with Sister Julie, came to us to tell us that we would have to leave her home the following day. We would no longer be able to stay there. I had no idea where I could take my wife and children. Just imagine being in a strange country, having no job, no home, no car, no money, and no friends or family—with people pursuing you with the intention of killing you and your family. Added to that was the issue of the AIDS pandemic. AIDS is a huge problem in South Africa. The people believed that if they contracted AIDS, they could be healed if they had sexual relations with a young child/baby/virgin. We were so concerned for our two young daughters. In addition, we had learned that every five minutes more than two hundred women were raped in South Africa. We had been invited to stay in a home, a safe place, until the shattering news came that we must leave. It would tear you apart. It tore us apart!

But, we mustered our courage and began praying, literally crying before the Lord. It seemed as if our prayers were going no further than the ceiling and bouncing back. We were not experiencing any breakthrough. Then the Holy Spirit started reminding me of the Word, how the blood of Jesus speaks better than the blood of Abel. He reminded me how Jesus took His own blood and presented it before the Father; and that blood, the blood of Jesus, speaks for us. I began to pray as Daniel prayed where he confessed the sins of his forefathers and his own sins. He asked that not for his righteousness, but for the sake of His mercies. So I began to pray in the same manner. "Lord, not for the sake of our righteousness, for our righteousness is as filthy rags, but for the sake of the blood of Jesus, which speaks better than the blood of Abel—let the blood of Jesus speak for us. We know that the blood of Jesus speaks for healing, deliverance, and miracles. "By mentioning the blood of Jesus, and asking God to let the blood of Jesus speak for us, we saw the heavens open, and a bright light came upon us. We saw Jesus in the glorious white clouds, sitting on the throne. His hand moved as though stamping a document or pounding a gavel, and He said, "It is done." Such a great joy came upon us. We began praising Jesus. We were reminded of His Word that says, "Ask and it will be given to you. Seek and you will find. Knock and the door will be opened to you" (Matthew 7:7 NKJV). "But without faith it is impossible to please him (God)" (Hebrews 11:6 KJV). "Therefore I say to you, whatever things you ask when you pray, believe that you receive them, and you will have them" (Mark 11:24 NKJV). Praise God! The experience with the Lord was so overwhelming that it was as though we were experiencing a great feast, and we were praising Him. All the fear and anxiety about tomorrow was gone!

But, later that evening, Satan tried to bring all kinds of doubts and fears to our minds, that it was just an illusion. "You are crazy. You will not get the visas for the United States. It is impossible. You are just deceiving yourselves." At the same time, the Lord reminded me of the story in 1 Kings when the Assyrians came to fight against Israel, and how God helped the Israelites to fight in the battle, and they defeated the Assyrians. The defeated army returned to their king and told him that the God of Israel was the God of the mountains, so the next year they would fight them in the plains and would defeat them. God sent the prophet to the Israelite king to tell him that because the Assyrians had decided that God was the God of the mountains, not of the plains, they would return the following year to fight in the plains; however, God would defeat them in the plains—proving that He is not only the God of the mountains, but the God of the plains also.

> Then the servants of the king of Syria said to him, "Their gods are gods of the hills. Therefore they were stronger than we; but if we fight against them in the plain, surely we will be stronger than they. So do this

thing: Dismiss the kings, each from his position, and put captains in their places; and you shall muster an army like the army that you have lost, horse for horse and chariot for chariot. Then we will fight against them in the plain; surely we will be stronger than they." And he listened to their voice and did so. So it was, in the spring of the year, that Ben-Hadad mustered the Syrians and went up to Aphek to fight against Israel. And the children of Israel were mustered and given provisions, and they went against them. Now the children of Israel encamped before them like two little flocks of goats, while the Syrians filled the countryside. Then a man of God came and spoke to the king of Israel, and said, 'Thus says the LORD: 'Because the Syrians have said, 'The LORD is God of the hills, but He is not God of the valleys,' therefore I will deliver all this great multitude into your hand, and you shall know that I am the LORD." (1 Kings 20:23–28 KJV)

Then the Lord reminded me of these passages in Daniel:

"Let his heart be changed from that of a man, let him be given the heart of a beast, and let seven times pass over him. 'This decision is by the decree of the watchers, and the sentence by the word of the holy ones, in order that the living may know that the Most High rules in the kingdom of men, gives it to whomever He will, and sets over it the lowest of men.' 'This dream I, King Nebuchadnezzar, have seen. Now you, Belteshazzar, declare its interpretation, since all the wise men of my kingdom are not able to make known to me the interpretation; but you are able, for the Spirit of the Holy God is in you'" (Daniel 4:16–18 NKJV).

"This is the interpretation, O king, and this is the decree of the Most High, which has come upon my lord the king: They shall drive you from men, your dwelling shall be with the beasts of the field, and they shall make you eat grass like oxen. They shall wet you with the dew of heaven, and seven times shall pass over you, till you know that the

Most High rules in the kingdom of men, and gives it to whomever He chooses. 'And inasmuch as they gave the command to leave the stump and roots of the tree, your kingdom shall be assured to you, after you come to know that Heaven rules'" (Daniel 4:24–26 NKJV).

"While the word was still in the king's mouth, a voice fell from heaven: 'King Nebuchadnezzar, to you it is spoken: the kingdom has departed from you! And they shall drive you from men, and your dwelling shall be with the beasts of the field. They shall make you eat grass like oxen; and seven times shall pass over you, until you know that the Most High rules in the kingdom of men, and gives it to whomever He chooses.' That very hour the word was fulfilled concerning Nebuchadnezzar; he was driven from men and ate grass like oxen; his body was wet with the dew of heaven till his hair had grown like eagles' feathers and his nails like birds' claws" (Daniel 4:31–33 NKJV).

"But when his heart was lifted up, and his spirit was hardened in pride, he was deposed from his kingly throne, and they took his glory from him. Then he was driven from the sons of men, his heart was made like the beasts, and his dwelling was with the wild donkeys. They fed him with grass like oxen, and his body was wet with the dew of heaven, till he knew that the Most High God rules in the kingdom of men, and appoints over it whomever He chooses. 'But you his son, Belshazzar, have not humbled your heart, although you knew all this'" (Daniel 5:20–22 NKJV).

And God spoke to my heart; He is the one who rules and reigns over the kingdoms of all mankind. He is the king over South Africa. He is the king over Pakistan. He is the king over the United States and over the entire world. I should not be afraid. He is going with me to the US Consulate. And, He is taking me to the United States. Praise God!

CHAPTER 29

The Visa Miracle

The next day, July 13, it was time to return to the US Consulate. Early in the morning, the church driver showed up to take us to the US Consulate. Thank God our host family did not come at that time to remove us from the home. We prayed again, asking God to go before us so that the officials would not ask any questions regarding our papers. The Lord reminded me that when Daniel was thrown into the lion's den, He closed the mouths of the lions: "My God sent His angel and shut the lions' mouths, so that they have not hurt me, because I was found innocent before Him; and also, O King, I have done no wrong before you" (Daniel 6:22 NKJV). He told us that He was going to close the mouths of the officials at the consulate! They would not ask any questions because He was going there with us.

As we approached the building, we invited Jesus to go with us. Though the enemy tried to frighten us, the Holy Spirit tenderly comforted us with the Word. And, as I remembered that I had invited Jesus to go with us, I knew His hand was in mine. We approached the window where there was a sign reading "U.S. Visas Picked up Here." The Holy Spirit was speaking to my heart: "Yes, you are going to pick up your passports with the US visa stamps on them." As we stood in line, I was experiencing both positive and negative feelings, despite the reassurances from the Lord. The negative feelings seemed to be rising up in power, but I was rebuking them and speaking the Word of God in my heart, over and over, to defeat those feelings. When our turn came to step up to the window, they returned our Pakistani passports, given to them three days before.

My hands were sweating and my legs were shaking. I found myself wanting desperately to open the passports to make sure the visa stamps were there, and yet still experiencing some fear. We stepped away from the window, and with sweaty/shaky hands opened the passports. There they were! Now, we were shaking with excitement! The Lord had once again gone before us and prepared the way where there was no way! We had our Pakistani passports stamped with three-year visas for the United States, without having submitted any of the required substantiating documents. Interestingly, our Pakistani passports were only valid for ten more days of travel. And yet, we had three-year visas for the United States! God ruled in our favor. We were rejoicing, though we still had no plane tickets.

We returned to Sister Julie's home. Before they could tell us to leave the home, we very quickly told them that we had obtained our US visas. They looked at us in a very doubtful way, and hesitantly said, "That is good news." We even called the pastor of the church and told him that we had been granted the visas for the United States. He was not even willing to believe that we had received them. I can understand why he doubted that we had them. We had just been told the day before that we had to leave the home they had arranged for us. He must have thought we had made up the story of the visas so that we would not be kicked out from that home. He sent a deacon to us, to make sure we were not lying about the visas. The deacon came and asked to see our passports. We gave them to him, and he checked every page, and even rubbed his hands over the pages as though he were checking to see if the passports and the visas were real. He carefully examined the dates of the passport expirations, the issue validation dates, and locations of the visas and every detail. He discovered that they were real. He was in awe and reported to the pastor that the visas were real.

According to our status with the South African government, on July 23, 1999, we would be deported back to Pakistan. Without God's intervention, we had just ten days until we would be sent back to Pakistan, where we would eventually be killed. And remember that we had been told we could no longer stay with the family where we had been staying. But when they saw that we obtained our visas for the United States, they said that we could stay a few more days until we obtained our plane tickets, and they became kinder to us.

As I mentioned before, we had no money, nor any credit card. In fact, in those days, I did not even know what a credit card looked like! I thank God that we did not have money or credit cards or any other visible resources to provide the funding for the tickets. I have since learned that credit cards have limits and can be declined. But I have Jesus! He has no limits! He never declines because He is faithful to do what He says He will do. And I was reminded of the vision we had seen, as His arm came down, and He said, "It is done."

We had to have those plane tickets before July 23. We received our visas for the United States on July 13, though they were stamped July 12, 1999. Not only would the South African government be after us for deportation back to Pakistan after the twenty-third, but also our Pakistani passports would expire that day and no longer be valid for travel. I called my father-in-law, who was living in the United States, and told him the good news that we had received our US visas. When he heard the news, he was very happy. I asked if he could help us with the purchase of the four plane tickets. He explained that he was in absolutely no position to help us. I am glad that my father-in-law was not able to help us. We had another opportunity for our faith to grow. The Holy Spirit was speaking to our hearts and telling us that the work that God starts, He always finishes. And as we trusted Him, He provided miraculously again and again. He also received all the glory! Hallelujah!

CHAPTER 30

Six Days and Counting

Remember that I shared about the church service we attended on July 4, 1999, and what the Lord spoke to me on that day. As we had listened to a South African couple announce their departure for the United States, the Lord instructed me not to come to church the following Sunday, but to stay home, fast and pray. Further, He said that the Sunday after that—July 18, we would be in the service and stand before the congregation to tell them that we also would be leaving for the United States. And here we were! It was just as He had spoken to me, exactly. And, remember that when He had spoken to me on the fourth, we did not have our US visas and had been told many times that we would not be able to obtain them! In fact, at that time I didn't even have any thought of returning to the US Consulate to reapply for the visas. The officials had angrily made it clear to us that we could not obtain US visas in South Africa with our Pakistani passports, and should not return to their office.

Now on July 18, we sat in that same church with our Pakistani passports stamped with the US visas! The pastor invited us to come in front of the congregation. He knew the story, the miracles of God's provision. He asked us to share our testimony. I shared about how God had made a way for us to get the US visas, and that we were going to the United States. I did not share with them concerning our urgent status with the South African government, our soon to expire Pakistani passports, or the time frame in which we would be leaving.

Two days later, on July 20, 1999, I heard the doorbell ring. I looked outside to see a tall man standing there. The man's name was Peter David. He said, "Pastor, I'd like to pray with you." We invited him in, and after he prayed with us, he opened his bag and said, "I brought these four plane tickets, booked, paid, and confirmed. You and your family are flying to the United States on July 22 at 6:00 p.m. on KLM, Northwest, and Continental Airlines! Your final destination will be Colorado Springs." In addition, he handed me $416 in cash and told me that the money was "for your Coke and Pepsi on the trip."

Praise the Lord! The Lord told me that He was going to take us to the United States like He took the people out of Egypt. We began thanking Him for protecting us through the attack in our hometown and through the many trials in South Africa. We thanked Him for making a way, time after time, where there was no way—providing homes for us to stay in, providing visas for us when we did not have the required documents and providing airline tickets to the United States. "Lord, You have done so much already. What more are you going to do?" Amazingly, He instructed me to read the book of Exodus and reminded me that when the Israelites left Egypt, they did not leave empty-handed: "And I will give this people favor in the sight of the Egyptians; and it shall be, when you go, that you shall not go empty-handed" (Exodus 3:21 NKJV). As we were preparing to leave for the airport, people came to say goodbye, and they gave us money. When we left South Africa, we had $1,900 US dollars.

Going to the Promised Land

As we were flying to the United States, I became fearful as I remembered what I had been told. People had said that when you arrive in the United States, the officials ask many questions—such as, where are you going to live? Who is going to sponsor you? What is your job going to be? All I knew was that our final destination was Colorado Springs. I did not even know that the United States had fifty states. I only knew that we were going to America and that there was a city called Colorado Springs.

We left Johannesburg, South Africa, and flew to Amsterdam. Our United States port of entry was Detroit, Michigan. As we approached the check-in points, there were four lines of people. Two lines were for citizens, and two lines were for noncitizens. We were standing in a short line, one for noncitizens. But the Lord spoke to my heart, instructing me to leave the short line and get in the longer line. So I told my wife, and we moved to the longer line. Sometimes, our faith can lead us to do crazy things! But you must listen to God, and when you do, you are safe. If we do not listen to His voice and obey, then we are in great danger. We stood in the longer line, and as our turn came to be processed, we approached the official, knowing that she would begin asking questions. But, she only asked one question, "What is your job going to be in the United States?"

At that very moment, the Lord spoke to my heart and told me, "Don't answer. I will speak for you." If you remember, when the Israelites came out of Egypt, they were on the shore of the Red Sea, with Pharaoh's army behind them. There was no way for them to escape. "And Moses said to the people, 'Do not be afraid. Stand still, and see the salvation of the LORD, which He will accomplish for you today. For the Egyptians whom you see today, you shall see again no more forever. The LORD will fight for you, and you shall hold your peace'" (Exodus 14:13–14 NKJV). So, after she asked about my work situation in the United States, and I did not answer for ten to fifteen seconds, she said, "Are you guys going to be missionaries in the United States?" Then I said, "Yes." She stamped our passports, and with a big smile said, "Welcome to the United States!"

Praise the Lord! We were in this beautiful and wonderful country. We arrived here on July 23, 1999. One of the most interesting and amazing things about our entry into the United States was that we were flying toward the West, not the East. The importance of that is that the time would have been different if we had been flying east. In other words, if we had been flying east our arrival date in the United States would have been July 24, 1999—one day after our Pakistani passports expired. It reminds me of how Joshua commanded the sun to stand still: "Then Joshua spoke to the LORD in the day when the LORD delivered up the Amorites before the children of Israel, and he said in the sight of Israel: 'Sun, stand still over Gibeon; and Moon, in the Valley of Aijalon.' So the sun stood still, and the moon stopped, till the people had revenge upon their enemies" (Joshua 10:12–13 NKJV). It was as though the Lord caused the sun to stand still so that we arrived in the United States on time, instead of one day late!

When we first received our plane tickets back in South Africa on July 20, 1999, I called my father-in-law, either that day or the next. I told him what the Lord Jesus Christ had done for us. I told him that He had provided the visas, plane tickets, and everything we needed to travel to the United States. "Please pray that we will not have any trouble with customs/immigration at the airport when we arrive in the United States."

We also told him that the final destination on the tickets was Colorado Springs. We told him that we did not know how far he was living from there. As I have already mentioned, I didn't even know that

127

there were fifty states in the United States, let alone any geographical understanding. I only knew that we were going to a city called Colorado Springs. We did know that our in-laws were living in Denver. We did not know that Denver and Colorado Springs were actually two cities within the same state. I asked my father-in-law, "How far is Denver from Colorado Springs? How will we be able to travel from Colorado Springs to Denver?" He laughed and told us with great joy, "God is really a miracle-working God! He is bringing you right next to us. Denver is just sixty-five miles from Colorado Springs! We will be very happy to come and get you at the airport."

CHAPTER 32

Reuniting in a New Land

What a joyous reunion it was as my wife's family met us at the airport in Colorado Springs! They took us to their home in Denver. In those days, they were living in a church apartment that had been given to them by the Redeemer Temple in Denver. Thank God for that church leadership! Pastor Lou Montecalvo and his team allowed us to stay with our family in the church apartment.

We were very overwhelmed as we rejoiced, praised the Lord, and reflected on all that He had done on our behalf!

One week after we arrived in the United States, we applied for our green cards. When we went to apply for the green cards, my father-in-law took me to the best attorney on immigration in Colorado. But she was also the most expensive attorney in Colorado! We learned that she was not a Christian. She did not even believe in God. And if you spoke on the phone with her for five minutes, you would be charged a seventy-five-dollar fee! We asked what she would charge to file our applications for the green cards. She said that the charge would be $4,800 for the four of us.

Do you remember that when we left South Africa for the United States, God spoke to my heart and said that He was taking us to the United States like the people of Israel? When I asked God what He meant by that, the Lord led me to Exodus, where He told Moses that when the Israelites left Egypt, they would not leave empty-handed, but rather would take the wealth of the Egyptians with them. When we were about to leave South Africa, we had $900 in US dollars and $1,000 in travelers' checks, for a total of $1,900. So I asked the attorney if I was required to pay the total amount all at one time, or if I could make payments. She said that I could make payments, but that I would have to make a down payment. I asked if she would accept the $1000 in travelers' checks as a down payment. She said yes. We gave her the checks, and she filed the applications.

The process had been started, but we had a balance of $3,800 to be paid to the attorney. Here we were in a new country, with no jobs and only $900 remaining. I gave $500 to my in-laws to purchase groceries and help with other household expenses. Then our remaining balance was $400! With that, we purchased baby food, diapers, and other needs for our children. Very quickly the remaining funds were gone. I was very worried because we had another payment due to the attorney the following month. We began to pray again! We cried out, "God we do not have any money to pay for the attorney fees, living expenses, or anything else. Please provide so that we are able to make our payment on time."

Remember that she was the most expensive attorney, and was not one who would accept untimely payments. We were praying. After one month, I received a bill from the attorney. The next payment of $200 was due. I didn't even have twenty dollars toward the bill, or to pay for anything else. I was afraid to even open the letter. But, when I opened it, I was in total awe and shock. It was not a bill, but a statement marked "PAID IN FULL"! Praise the Lord!

When we first arrived in the United States, and saw the situation here, things seemed dark. My father-in-law's family was living in the church apartment, and they did not have much to share with us, but we were so grateful for their hospitality and kindness.

While we were grateful to be in a safe place, to be reunited with family, we were also feeling like all the doors were closed. It was as though we had left Egypt, faced the Red Sea, survived the wilderness, crossed the Jordan River, and now we were facing the walls of Jericho!

As the clock ticked away the time in South Africa, moving us closer and closer to the threat of being returned to Pakistan, God intervened and brought us out of "Egypt"!

The first leg of our flight to the United States was from Johannesburg, South Africa, to Amsterdam. As we waited at the gate in Amsterdam to board the plane for the United States, the immigration authorities took our passports. Then they left with them! We began to pray, "Dear Lord God, please have mercy." After more than thirty minutes, the authorities returned, handed us our passports and said, "Okay, now you can board your plane." That was our "Red Sea"!

When we faced customs in Detroit, Michigan, we were standing at our "River Jordan."

And, as we discovered our difficult circumstances after arriving in Colorado, we realized that this was our "Jericho."

And, once again, God led my wife to pray and fast for three days. As she prayed, God gave her a dream. In her dream, she saw the word *Philadelphia*. When she got up in the morning, she was asking herself what the significance of *Philadelphia* might be.

Then the Lord led her to the third chapter of Revelation. She read verses 7 through 12 about the message to the church at Philadelphia. Then the Lord made very clear to her that verses 7 and 8 were directly for us. "And to the angel of the church in Philadelphia write, 'These things says He who is holy, He who is true, "He who has the key of David, He who opens and no one shuts, and shuts and no one opens": "I know your works. See, I have set before you an open door, and no one can shut it; for you have a little strength, have kept My word, and have not denied My name."' (NKJV)

Just as God appeared to Joshua in the Jericho valley, as the captain of the host, the same God came and gave my wife the word that He had an open door before us that no man would be able to close. Praise Him! When my wife shared what the Lord had spoken to her, we both were so encouraged and blessed. We praised God for His words of comfort, and we knew that He was going to open a door for us here. He had brought us with His mighty power this far. He would not let us down now.

CHAPTER 33

A New Life in a New Land

We began settling in to life here in the United States. It was increasingly difficult for us to stay with my in-laws in their small, one bedroom apartment. Often, my wife and I slept on the floor, but we were happy. We felt safe and had no fear of being deported. We began to pray and ask, "Please, Lord God, provide a place of our own where we can have more space."

After one year of living with my in-laws, with nine of us in that little apartment, we were introduced to an organization called Colorado Homeless Families, led by a wonderful, loving, and godly Christian sister, Connie Zimmerman. Thank God, they arranged for us to have a three-bedroom condominium at very low rent (about $150 per month, instead of the usual $1,200). The condominium even had a garage! We also learned of a local food bank where we were not only able to get food to feed our family, but I was also able to work there. Some of the income I earned helped us with our living expenses, and part of it was credited toward our rent payment. God again was providing in miraculous ways.

We eventually began praying for a car. I was reminded of when we were still in South Africa. I had been praying for a car, and, one day, a man came to me and told me that he wanted to give me a car. At that time, I told him, "I very much appreciate your offer. But I am sorry I cannot accept because I do not know how to drive."

Now, here we were in the United States, and we were once again praying for a car! We prayed for a car for about six months. One day the

Lord spoke to me softly and gently, "I cannot give you a car because you need to learn how to drive first." I said, "Lord, why didn't you tell me that sooner?" Of course, it was not God's fault! It was my own fault; I should have known that I needed a license to drive! I was so thankful to Him for the reminder that I needed to learn to drive first.

On the very same day that the Lord spoke to me regarding my need to learn to drive, I asked my brother-in-law Stephen how it would be possible for me to learn to drive a car. I asked if he could teach me. He told me that before he would teach me, I needed to have a permit. And in order to get a permit, I needed to go to the Department of Motor Vehicles, where they would give me a book with the rules and regulations for driving. After I studied the book, I could go back and take the exam. When I passed the exam, they would give me a permit, and then Stephen would teach me to drive. So, I got the book and read it for one week, and then returned to take the exam. I passed the test. Then Stephen and my sister-in-law, Hannah, began taking turns teaching me to drive.

After two weeks of driving lessons, I received a phone call from Faith Harvest Church in Mesa, Arizona. Pastor Mark and Maggie Hillis asked me to come and speak in their church on a Sunday morning. They sent me the roundtrip plane ticket to Phoenix. I preached in their church and God moved and touched the people. They were really blessed. They arranged for me to speak in another church, Calvary Chapel in Mesa, that evening. When I spoke that evening, even before I stepped down from the pulpit, the pastor of Calvary Chapel Church, Pastor Charlie, came and stood beside me. He asked the congregation to stand and stretch their hands toward me. He asked if there was anything that I needed prayer for. "Please pray with me as I am praying that God will provide transportation for us, in the form of a car." When I said that, Pastor Charlie said, "We are not going to pray for this thing!"

I was really surprised and a bit confused. I was thinking to myself, *He asked me what my prayer needs were because they were going to pray, and then said they would not pray for that very thing!* Then he said to the congregation, "Keep on standing and keep stretching your hands. Let me go into my office and I will come right back." He came back a minute or two later with a car key in his hand. He told the congregation, "When I said we were not going to pray for a car, it is because God has already answered. He has already provided a car. Here is the key and the title to the car God has provided." The key was for a 1995 Nissan Sentra! Praise Jesus!

I learned something through this process. When you are praying for something, God is not going to answer your prayer until you move to the level where you can handle the blessing properly, and only for His glory. As I was sharing with you, God did not give me the car until I learned how to drive a car! In the same way, God will not bless us with something if we are not prepared to receive it.

It took two years to get the green cards, so we were very thankful that we had three-year visas. We obtained our green cards in November 2001. And by January 25, 2008, we all became United States citizens! *When God starts something, He always finishes it! He finishes it even before He starts it!*

CHAPTER 34

What Shall We Do, Lord?

My wife and I had continued, from the time we arrived in the United States, praying that God would open a door for ministry. My wife even fasted again for three days and three nights without food and water in August 1999, for our ministry. While we were still living in my in-laws' apartment, I was introduced to a man from Promise Keepers. He had started a weekly telephone prayer conference call every Wednesday at 4:00 p.m. He invited me to join the call. I did not have many opportunities for ministry at that time, so it seemed like a good idea to become part of this prayer call. Shortly after I joined the prayer call, the man who had started it shared that they were going to have a Promise Keepers conference in Arizona. So I rode with him to the conference. When we arrived, we stayed with some of his family members. The next day we went to the conference, being held in the Arizona Diamondbacks Stadium.

The Promise Keepers event was so overwhelming to me. I had never seen so many Christians gathered together in one place. It was really a good conference. As I was visiting some of the exhibition booths of different ministries represented there, I noticed one from a mission organization called Voice of the Martyrs. I had never heard of this group before. I met a brother named Alan at that booth. He was from Romania. I spoke with him, and he asked where I was from. I told him that I was from Pakistan. He asked what things were like in Pakistan. I told him my story, and about the persecution in my home country. Then he asked for my contact information and told me that he would like me to come and speak in some Romanian churches in the Sacramento, California, area where he lived.

We returned to Colorado a few days later. My brother-in-law John took me to another conference in Colorado. During a break in the conference, I was sitting outside enjoying the sunshine, and this couple came to me and asked who I was and where I came from. I told them that I was a Christian pastor from Pakistan. They invited me to join them for supper that evening. That evening I learned that the man was the manager of the Daystar Christian television station in Denver. He told me that he would like me to speak on his television program. Later that week, I appeared on his program, and I spoke about the persecuted church.

A week after speaking on his program, a brother from Voice of the Martyrs, David Witt, spoke on his program. When David Witt spoke, he mentioned my hometown, which had been burned on February 6, 1997. Then, Brother Ruben Mendez, the Daystar manager, told him that he should meet the brother from Pakistan who had spoken on his program the week before. So, the brother from VOM called me and told the VOM leadership about me. I praise God! That is how I was introduced to the ministry of Voice of the Martyrs.

For the last fifteen years, I have been preaching and teaching here in the United States, in churches, schools, colleges and universities, home groups, and wherever God opens a door. He has called me to warn my American brothers and sisters about the dangers of Islam, and to encourage them to be educated about Islam. The Bible says, "My people are destroyed for lack of knowledge" (Hosea 4:6a NKJV).

A military general said, "If you want to defeat your enemy, you must know everything about them—what they think, what they eat—everything about them. It will then be easy for you to defeat them."

I want to make it clear here that I am not encouraging you to go and physically fight against the Muslims. Muslims are not our enemies. Those who follow Islam are deceived by Satan. They are lost. Muslims are our responsibility. The war we are being called to engage in is a spiritual one. I am asking that you stand for the Truth of the gospel of

Jesus Christ and that you stand against false religions. I challenge you to become educated of the truth about Islam, and that you learn how to share the gospel with Muslims so that they might be set free and discover the assurance of eternal life.

As you have read my story, you must have been blessed that God gave us victory over all the trials and tribulations. Yes, God has given us great victory in bringing us safely to the United States. But if He had not brought us here, we would still worship Him, because we are still victorious, still more than conquerors.

One time when I was preaching in Arizona, God gave me a word for the United States. He told me that He had called me to this nation like the prophet Jeremiah. The Lord told Jeremiah to warn the people of Israel, "For thus says the LORD: 'Behold, I will make you a terror to yourself and to all your friends; and they shall fall by the sword of their enemies, and your eyes shall see it. I will give all Judah into the hand of the king of Babylon, and he shall carry them captive to Babylon and slay them with the sword. Moreover I will deliver all the wealth of this city, all its produce, and all its precious things; all the treasures of the kings of Judah I will give into the hand of their enemies, who will plunder them, seize them, and carry them to Babylon. And you, Pashhur, and all who dwell in your house, shall go into captivity. You shall go to Babylon, and there you shall die, and be buried there, you and all your friends, to whom you have prophesied lies'" (Jeremiah 20:4–6 NKJV).

As God spoke to my heart, I became so afraid for the American people, as well as for my family and myself. I was really worried because too many people in America are sleeping. They are so concerned about being politically correct that they are not willing to speak the truth. They are very much afraid of the Muslims, and are not willing to speak negatively about Islam. It began even before September 11, 2001. President Clinton said that Islam is a religion of peace. Following that, President Bush said several times that Islam was a peace-loving religion. Condoleeza Rice said Islam is a peace-loving religion. Presidents, congressmen, and other high-ranking government officials have said the same.

They have all gone too far! I have a copy of a video where President

137

George W. Bush even said that we worship the same god, we just have different routes of getting there, and that Muslims will also go to heaven. People think that all of these leaders are more educated and patriotic, so they must be telling the truth.

Again, I want to emphasize and challenge you to become educated for yourself. Do not quickly accept whatever our leaders say, or the media proclaims or even implies. Pursue truth, not political correctness. And to pursue truth, we must go to the source or sources. We must look to the Bible to learn the truth of Christianity. We must look to the Qur'an and the Hadith (and other Muslim writings) to learn the truth about Islam. (See appendix 2, "Allah, the god of the Qur'an vs. Yahweh, the God of the Bible.")

CHAPTER 35

Seek God's Choice

I had an opportunity to meet a lady, a former Miss Alabama, who was once married to a Muslim. She shared that the Syrian man she had married had been wonderful from the day they met until the day they married. When they were dating, he was so romantic, caring, thoughtful, and attentive to her needs. He made her feel loved and cared for. She believed he was the most amazing man in the world. They were married in the mosque, and then her world was turned upside down. He became physically abusive, controlling, and unloving. That is the story of more than 90 percent of the women who marry Muslims—young women convinced that Muslim men are the most wonderful, the most caring, the most romantic, the most loving that you would ever meet— so much more so than any American man. When they are dating, they are encouraged to believe and are convinced that women are held in the highest esteem in the Qur'an and that Muslim men who desire to be obedient to Allah will honor their women and care for them with great tenderness and love. (See appendix 6: "Women in Islam")

When she married in the mosque, she did not even know that she was given a Muslim name and was led in reading the Islamic creed. In doing so, she was then declared a Muslim. Prior to marriage, she was told that she could raise her children in the Christian faith, but after marrying her Muslim husband, she was told that she could not even speak the name of Jesus in her home.

She shared that her ex-husband and former brother-in-law both said that if Muslims were not able to take the United States by force, they would take this country by marriage! She also said that when she saw the pictures of the 9/11 hijackers, she was stunned. Of the nineteen hijackers in the photos, fifteen of them had visited her home in Florida many times.

In her book, *Married to Mohammed*, W. L. Cati shares that almost ten thousand American girls are marrying Muslim men every year, and then converting to Islam. That is a very scary number and is of great concern to me.

Many times young women are at my presentations. I remind them about the sins of the Israelites: "Thus the children of Israel dwelt among the Canaanites, the Hittites, the Amorites, the Perizzites, the Hivites, and the Jebusites. And they took their daughters to be their wives, and gave their daughters to their sons; and they served their gods. So the children of Israel did evil in the sight of the LORD. They forgot the LORD their God, and served the Baals and Asherahs"(Judges 3:5–7 NKJV). The Bible makes it very clear in 2 Corinthians 6:14 (NKJV): "Do not be unequally yoked together with unbelievers. For what fellowship has righteousness with lawlessness? And what communion has light with darkness?"

I also tell them, "Please remember that God is your provider, not a Muslim man—or any man. Do not marry a Muslim even if he offers you the world. Remember God is your provider." Then I share my own experience.

Remember that when I was first saved, I did not become a preacher right away. I wrestled with God for a while before submitting! At that time, I was working in a factory. One day a Muslim businessman approached me and began asking me questions. He asked how old I was and what my educational background was. He also asked me about my faith. I answered his questions and told him that I was a Christian. He protested, "Christians should not be that educated."I told him that anyone can be educated. It is not a Christian or a Muslim thing. In a way he was right, because in Pakistan Christians are very poor. Most cannot afford to go to school or pursue higher education.

The Muslim businessman then asked me to become a Muslim. I

told him that I would not become a Muslim. He offered me his business and said that both of his daughters could be my wives. But I refused and told him that I would never ever do such a thing. "I am a Christian and I will remain a Christian no matter what someone offers me." I thank God that He protected me that day, and helped me to take a firm and strong stand for my Christian faith. The offer of wealth or women did not tempt me.

Today I am very blessed to have a wonderful, godly Christian wife. I praise God that He has blessed me with children, and there is no conflict between me and my wife. We are raising our children together in a godly environment. When we refuse to listen to God, and follow money and the things of the world, we suffer.

Remember the story of Abraham. Abraham was living in the land of Israel, and a famine took place. Abraham learned that there was food in Egypt, so he decided to go to Egypt. He did not ask God whether he should go. It was his plan to go there. On the way to Egypt he told his wife Sarah to lie and say that she was his sister instead of his wife. When Abraham and Sarah went to Egypt, Sarah was taken by the Pharaoh to be his wife. God intervened in the situation and brought Sarah back to Abraham. When Sarah was returned to Abraham, the Pharaoh sent her with gifts, servants, and maidservants. One of the gifts was Hagar, the Egyptian maidservant. Today we are facing the consequences from the children of Ishmael, all over the world. If Abraham had sought God's counsel, and had not gone to Egypt, the door would not have been opened that brought Hagar and then Ishmael.

If Abraham had asked God whether or not he should go to Egypt, God may have told him that He would provide for their needs in another way. Abraham chose not to seek God's counsel, and opened the door for the enemy to work. When God told Isaac not to go to Egypt when there was another famine in the land, Isaac planted and reaped a hundredfold harvest! Note that not only did Abraham not ask God about whether he should go to Egypt, he also instructed his wife to lie. Because of his choices, he opened the door for his wife to be taken. Abraham did not trust God for his provision but chose to go to Egypt without asking Him.

It is the same way today. The ten thousand American girls who are marrying Muslim men every year are not asking God if it is His plan for their lives, not trusting Him to be their provider. Rather, like Abraham, they are deciding on their own what they want and trusting the Muslim men for their provision.

Please follow along with me and think about this. If Abraham had asked God whether or not he should go to Egypt, and he was obedient when God told him not to go because He would provide, Sarah would not have been taken into Pharaoh's harem. Hagar would not have been sent as Sarah's maid when Sarah was returned to Abraham. Further, if Sarah and Abraham had continued to trust God to provide their descendants, rather than taking matters into their own hands, Ishmael would not have been born. Finally, if Ishmael had not been born, we would not have Islam!

In our present day, a girl from Kansas married a Muslim man from Kenya. She gave birth to a boy, and then her husband left her. She later married another Muslim man from Indonesia. He took his wife and stepson to Indonesia. That little boy spent several years being educated in the Muslim school. Most of his evenings were spent in the mosque memorizing the Qur'an. The woman eventually returned to the United States with her son. In 2008, her son became the President of the United States (above information is taken from *Obama Nation*, by Jerome R. Corsi). I remember before the election in 2008, the Lord showed me that if Obama was elected as President of the United States, God was unleashing His judgment on this nation. (For more information about Obama's plan for this nation, I encourage you to watch the documentary *2016*, by DineshD'Souza).

I recommend to my readers that if you are a father or mother, please educate your daughters about the vital importance of trusting God as their provider and seeking Him for His choice for a life partner. Educate them with the truth about Islam and the Islamic agenda that includes making inroads into this nation through marriage. Failing to do so will not only bring destruction to them, but can also advance the destruction of our whole nation.

It is very common, almost throughout the world, for people to seek mates who are wealthy and/or influential. The perceived benefits of making such an alliance, as well as the charm of the pursuer, can be so enticing and seemingly irresistible. But, as followers of Jesus Christ, we trust His Word. We must seek His guidance and trust Him to provide. And His Word promises: "Now to Him who is able to do exceedingly abundantly above all that we ask or think, according to the power that works in us" (Ephesians 3:20 NKJV). His plan for our lives is: "For I know the thoughts that I think toward you, says the LORD, thoughts of peace and not of evil, to give you a future and a hope" (Jeremiah 29:11 KJV).

Ninety-five percent of couples do not marry the person that God has chosen for them; instead, they follow their own desires. As you read this book, ask yourself this question: if you are married, did you really pray and fast about whom you should be marrying? If you are single, I would strongly encourage you to pray and fast about whether or not your potential partner is from God or if it is just your own desire.

CHAPTER 36

What if ...?

I praise God that I married a good, godly Christian woman. Over the years, she has fasted ten times like Queen Esther in the Bible fasted, for three days and three nights without food or water. She prays with me and for me. I praise God that the offer extended to me by that Muslim businessman all those years ago in Pakistan did not persuade me. Just imagine if I had listened to him, had rejected Jesus Christ and had married his daughters. I would not be part of the Kingdom of the Lord Jesus Christ. I would have no assurance of my salvation.

Faith Covenant International, also known as *Cry of the Persecuted Church*, would not exist. We would not be seeing thousands of people giving their lives to Jesus in Pakistan, through the ministry that we have today. We would not have a program to support the poor children in Pakistan, to pay their school fees and provide for their other needs. There would not have been the Jesus Heals Medical Clinic where thousands of people received free medical care in the name of Jesus Christ. The many Christian families who have been freed through the ministry would still be enslaved in the brick kilns of Pakistan. There would not be hope that more will be freed. There would be no Faith Covenant Bible School, which has graduated hundreds of students since 2000.

If I had made that wrong choice, I would still hate Israel, India, and the West. I would not have gone to India to preach the Gospel of the Lord Jesus Christ, resulting in 103 churches planted there, as of this writing. We would not have seen the starting of thirty-five Bible schools in Sri Lanka. I would not have traveled to South Africa for Bible College, or returned years later to encourage believers there and see a church planted. I would not have seen the birthing of a church in the United Arab Emirates. I would not have seen hundreds of people saved and healed in Rwanda and Uganda, and the beginnings of church planting efforts there. (I believe we will see all of Africa and Asia reached with the Gospel of the Lord Jesus Christ.) I would not have shared the Gospel message, the story of His faithfulness and power, with hundreds of thousands of Americans.

Had I made the wrong choice, God would have called another because we know He will accomplish His will on the earth. How I praise Him! By the power of the Holy Spirit, I was able to make the right choice. There are so many things, so many ways in which God has blessed me because I chose well—standing for Jesus, and then marrying a Christian woman.

In this very moment, as you are holding this book in your hand, I believe that these stories have blessed your life. You would not have received this blessing if I had made the wrong choice. But, praise God! He helped me to make the right choice. Today as you are reading this book, I trust that you are being blessed, and I rejoice in that. Please make the right choices and encourage others around you to choose well and choose Jesus.

I also want to share with you that for the last twenty-three years, I have been following Christ. I cannot say, nor would I dare to say, that I am perfect. Many times I have made mistakes. But God has always provided for me. There has not been a single day when I have gone to sleep hungry, or have not had a roof over my head. Sometimes I have had much, sometimes little. I may not have everything I want, but God has blessed me with everything I need. As the apostle Paul writes in his letter to the Philippians: "Not that I speak in regard to need, for I have learned in whatever state I am, to be content: I know how to be abased, and I know how to abound. Everywhere and in all things I have learned both to be full and to be hungry, both to abound and to suffer need.

I can do all things through Christ who strengthens me" (Philippians 4:11–13 NKJV).

I trusted Jesus rather than the Muslim businessman, and He has never let me down! The Bible says that cursed is the one who trusts in man. Don't be cursed! Be blessed by trusting in Jesus instead of trusting in man. Man may die, his business may fail, but Jesus will live forever, and there is no lack in His Kingdom. Throughout His Word, the Lord promises that He will not abandon us and that He will provide for us:

"For He Himself has said, 'I will never leave you nor forsake you'" (Hebrews 13:5b NKJV).

"Be strong and of good courage, do not fear nor be afraid of them; for the Lord your God, He is the One who goes with you. He will not leave you nor forsake you … And the Lord, He is the One who goes before you. He will be with you. He will not leave you nor forsake you; do not fear nor be dismayed" (Deuteronomy 31:6, 8 NKJV).

"No man shall be able to stand before you all the days of your life; as I was with Moses, so I will be with you. I will not leave you nor forsake you" (Joshua 1:5 NKJV).

"The LORD is my shepherd; I shall not want. He makes me to lie down in green pastures; He leads me beside the still waters. He restores my soul; He leads me in the paths of righteousness for His name's sake. Yea, though I walk through the valley of the shadow of death, I will fear no evil; for You are with me; Your rod and Your staff, they comfort me. You prepare a table before me in the presence of my enemies; You anoint my head with oil; my cup runs over. Surely goodness and mercy shall follow me all the days of my life; and I will dwell in the house of the LORD forever" (Psalm 23 NKJV).

"Do not put your trust in princes, nor in a son of man, in whom there is no help. His spirit departs, he returns to his earth; in that very day his plans perish. Happy is he who has the God of Jacob for his help, whose hope is in the Lord his God, Who made heaven and earth, the sea, and all that is in them. Who keeps truth forever, who executes justice for the oppressed, who gives food to the hungry? The Lord gives freedom to the prisoners. The Lord opens the eyes of the blind; the Lord raises those who are bowed down; the Lord loves the righteous. The

Lord watches over the strangers; He relieves the fatherless and widow; but the way of the wicked He turns upside down. The Lord shall reign forever—Your God, O Zion, to all generations. Praise the Lord!" (Psalm 146:3–10 NKJV).

I am so wonderfully blessed, and I praise God. I am especially grateful because of the choice to follow Christ, the right choice. One day, when I leave this earth, I am 100 percent sure that I will go to heaven, where I will see my Jesus face to face. And, through the doors God has opened for me and our ministry team, we believe that there will be millions upon millions who will also go to heaven.

It is very important for us to realize that no matter what mistakes we have made, how many sins we have committed, when we make the right choice … when we choose to follow the Lord Jesus Christ, He can and will use us for His glory. The story of Paul's conversion in the ninth chapter of Acts is a wonderful reminder of His amazing power to transform lives and use anyone. Paul had been one of the key leaders, influencing others to persecute and kill followers of Christ. But God had a different plan for Paul's life. In His grace, He offered Paul (Saul) a choice. Paul chose well. He chose to accept the Lord Jesus Christ, for who He really is, the longed-for Messiah. Consider this; we will not know the full impact of Paul's ministry as a follower of Christ until Jesus returns!

In His grace, He gave me a choice, just as He gives each of you a choice. When I said yes, He began to move on my behalf, performing countless miracles of healing, provision, and deliverance. Again and again, He made ways where there were none. He brought us through all the persecution and trials in our homeland, carried us through the challenges and tribulations during our time in South Africa, and then delivered us safely here in the United States. He then began to reveal His purposes in bringing us here.

He connected us with the ministry of the Voice of the Martyrs. How we thank God for Pastor Richard Wurmbrand, who founded VOM. There are so many wonderful brothers and sisters serving with VOM, many as volunteers. They blessed us with their help, encouragement, and prayers.

Praise the Lord! Voice of the Martyrs began to endorse me and our ministry, Faith Covenant International/Cry of the Persecuted Church, through letters of introduction to churches. Since 2001, I have traveled throughout this nation. I have visited forty-six of the fifty states. By the grace of God, I have spoken in more than one thousand churches, and in Bible schools, colleges and universities, and many conferences.

Doors have opened for ministry in India, Rwanda, South Africa, Sri Lanka, United Arab Emirates, United Kingdom, Nigeria, and Uganda. The Lord continues to make new connections and open new doors, surprising us again and again with His amazing ways. We continue to be overwhelmed and humbled. He is so faithful, so gracious, so merciful, so loving. We praise Him.

CHAPTER 37

Thoughts to Consider

Several years ago, I had an opportunity to watch the movie *Gandhi.* I was surprised to learn that he carried a New Testament in his pocket at all times. He was very much inspired by the teachings of the Lord Jesus Christ. Many of Gandhi's sayings are taken from the teachings of Jesus. For example, he says, "Be the change you wish to see in the world." I know those are the words of Jesus as He said, "And just as you want men to do to you, you also do to them likewise" (Luke 6:31 NKJV).

While traveling by train to Pretoria, Gandhi experienced his first taste of racial discrimination. In spite of carrying first-class tickets, he was indiscriminately thrown out of the train by the authorities on the instigation of a white man. Later I read that one time Gandhi had gone to a Christian church in Pretoria. "The church did not make a favorable impression on me. The sermon seemed to be uninspiring. The congregation did not strike me as being particularly religious. They were not an assembly of devout souls. They appeared rather to be a worldly-minded people, going to church for recreation and in conformity to custom. During the service, I would sometimes involuntarily dose. I was ashamed, but some of those sitting around me did the same! I could not go on long like this and soon gave up attending the service." Gandhi approached another church to attend services, only to be barred from entering by one of the deacons standing at the door. Just imagine! If that church had shown the love of Jesus Christ to Gandhi, how might the picture of India today be different?

Mahatma Gandhi is one of the most respected leaders of modern history. A Hindu, Ghandi nevertheless admired Jesus and often quoted from the Sermon on the Mount. Once, when the missionary E. Stanley Jones met with Ghandi, he asked him, "Mr. Ghandi, though you quote the words of Christ often, why is it that you appear to so adamantly reject becoming his follower?" Ghandi replied, "Oh, I don't reject your Christ. I love your Christ. It's just that so many of you Christians are so unlike your Christ."

How we treat others tells people *more* about what we believe, and what following Jesus means to us than all the tracts we pass out, or all the fine sermons we deliver.

God may bring someone into your life that may be poor or in need. I remember a story I was told when I was in a meeting. There was a woman who was praying and asking, "Jesus, I want to see you. Please come and visit me." One day Jesus spoke to her and told her, "I am going to come and visit you at 1:00 p.m., and I will have lunch with you." She now knew the date and time. She was so excited. She began preparing, cleaning her house, and making it ready for her special visitor. When the day came for His visit, she was impatiently waiting for Him to come. The bell rang an hour before the expected arrival time. She ran to the door thinking He must be early. As she opened the door, she saw a homeless man who was very dirty and wearing ragged clothes. He humbly asked if she could spare some bread for him because he had not eaten anything since the day before. She was so angry and shouted at him. "I cannot help you. This is not a good time. My Jesus is coming for a visit. He will be here very soon. Just go away."

Many times we say that we love Jesus, but the Bible says that if we do not love our fellow man, we cannot love Jesus. The woman in the story I heard gave nothing to the beggar and sent him away. "But whoever has this world's goods, and sees his brother in need, and shuts up his heart from him, how does the love of God abide in him?" (1 John 3:17 NKJV). Her story is not finished—the woman closed the door and anxiously awaited the visitor she had been longing to see, pacing the floor. Finally the clock struck 1:00 p.m., the time she had been longing for. But He did not come. She waited for almost another hour, but still He did not come. She began praying, "Jesus, you promised that you would be here today at 1:00 p.m., but you did not come. What happened?"

She heard the voice of Jesus say, "I did come, but you shouted at me, told me to leave and slammed the door in my face." She responded, "Jesus, that was a beggar, not you." Then Jesus reminded her about His words in Matthew 25. The lesson for us to take away from this story is that many times God brings people across our paths, but because we have our own ideas about what it means to serve, we miss the opportunity because of reasons such as: "I don't speak that brother's language, so I can't serve him"; "That person is not as educated as me, nor does he have the same background, nor does he attend the same church as me"; "His skin is a different color." Sometimes we make these things so important, even more important than Jesus Christ Himself. Billy Graham said, "If you really want to see an example of racism, you can see it on Sunday."

I do not intend to offend anyone here, but I want to share a personal experience. I was invited to a mission's conference—"Reach to the Nations of the World for Jesus"—in Johannesburg while we were still in South Africa. When I arrived there, the director of the conference met me. He was very happy to see me. He said, "Pastor, we welcome you here to this conference. You are our international guest. Here is your name badge. It is a VIP badge. You will not be eating with the local pastors and people, but you will be eating upstairs with the international guests and speakers." I replied to him, "Pastor, don't worry about this VIP badge. I will eat with the local people downstairs." He was so insistent that there was no way to turn the VIP badge down.

Later, when I went upstairs to eat with the international guests and speakers, it did go very well. All of them were white. I was the only one of color. The next day, I went to eat my lunch upstairs, as I had been directed to do. I was in the middle of my lunch when the director's secretary came to me and said that I could not and should not be in the dining room. I tried to explain to her that I had been instructed by her boss to do so. She refused to listen to me, and told me that I was not allowed to eat there because I was not a white person. I went downstairs with the food plate in my hand, weeping as I went. I later told the director, but he did not seem to care what his own secretary had done. As I thought about that painful experience, I questioned how they expected to reach the nations for Jesus with that kind of attitude.

Even here in the United States, many times I have seen that kind of discrimination and prejudice. On three occasions after September 11, 2001, I was given traffic tickets when I had not made any mistake. One time when I mistakenly pulled into a no parking zone, a white police officer in Florida shouted, "Go back to the country where you came from." This was in June 2010, after I had been a United States citizen for more than two years. A number of times, people, even those who call themselves Christian, even those who are serving in ministries, have insulted me in front of others. One time I was denied a haircut because I looked Middle Eastern! I am not angry at any non-Christians who behave in such a way. I expect that kind of behavior from non-Christians. But, when Christians, those who claim to be mission leaders and directors, serving in positions of influence and leadership, behave in that way, it is hurtful and so disappointing. I am so grateful that Jesus modeled how we should respond as He prayed on the cross, "Father, forgive them for they don't know what they are doing." I pray that God will bless them and set them free from the bondage of racism.

As a white person reading this book, you may not understand the pain I am describing. If you are a person of color reading this book, it will be very easy for you to identify with what I have shared. Ever since arriving in this country, I have heard that here we have freedom of religion and freedom of speech, and I do believe that this is the best country in the world. I love this country, and I mean that with all of my heart. I have told many of my American brothers and sisters that I love this country more than they do. I grew up in a country where there was no freedom of religion and no freedom of speech.

When we came to the United States, we did gain the freedom of speech and freedom of religion, but we lost the freedom of color. Here, when I travel with my family and have booked a hotel, I leave my family in the car while I go in to register. My experience has taught me that when we all go in together; we are given inferior rooms with poor views, etc., because they are saving the best rooms for others. I travel almost every week, and because of so much air travel, I sometimes am upgraded from economy to first class. Previously, when I knew that I should be upgraded, and approached the counter to ask about the upgrade, and they saw me and knew my name, they purposely removed my name from the list of those who would be upgraded. So now I no longer even go to the counter. I simply wait for my name to be called or to be shown on the screen. I confess that I am afraid that if I ask, I will lose my chance to be upgraded.

Just imagine! We are not welcome in the country where I was born. If we were to return, we might be killed because of our faith in Jesus Christ. And we are not even welcome here because of the color of our skin. So I more desperately pray for the kingdom of the Lord Jesus Christ to come, so that we all might be free from the evil of man.

I invited a preacher I had known in South Africa—we stayed in his home four months—to come to the United States. When he came here, I hosted him in my home for one month, and arranged church meetings for him where he could speak. One day he told me that he wanted to confess something to me. I asked him, "What?" He said, "When you stayed in my home, I used to look down upon you. I never thought that one day you would be helping me. Now, I have learned that I should never underestimate any person, any time. You never know when God may bring that person you have looked down upon to help you."

I was reminded of when we were in Tongaat, South Africa. As poor people from Pakistan, we were looked down upon, even by the Christians. The pastor in the church there asked that I be at the church every day, although I had nothing to do. One day a woman came to the church with her daughter who was being tormented by demons. The pastors began to pray for the girl, though they did not invite me to join them. They prayed for quite a while, but the torment continued. Finally, they asked me to pray. As I prayed the blood of Jesus over the girl, she fell to the floor and was delivered in that moment. It was such an important lesson for me. When someone is in need, I must not take advantage of that person or think less of him or her because he or she is needy. I was hurt when the pastors did not invite me to join them in ministering to the girl. But the Lord used that situation to teach me to respect those in authority, even when it seemed unfair, and to trust Him more to move on my behalf.

"After these things I looked, and behold, a great multitude which no one could count, from every nation and all tribes and peoples and tongues, standing before the throne and before the Lamb, clothed in white robes, and palm branches were in their hands; and they cry out with a loud voice, saying, 'Salvation to our God who sits on the throne, and to the Lamb'" (Revelation 7:9–10 NASB).

Heaven will reflect people from every tongue, tribe and nation. How awesome it would be, and how honored God would be, if we saw the coming together of every tongue, tribe, and nation right here on earth, even before Jesus returns, even before heaven.

CHAPTER 38

Loving the Lost

In 2015, the Lord helped me fast for many days. At the end of the year, I counted the days that I had fasted and found the number to be a hundred days. On July 23, 2015, it was my forty-ninth day of fast when the Lord gave me a similar experience to Paul, as stated in 2 Corinthians 12:21. The Lord allowed me to go to Heaven, and he also allowed me to see Hell on three different occasions. After seeing my family members, especially my mother, in Hell, God has given me a deep passion to pray for the lost. After having the vision of Hell, I didn't want anyone, not even my worst enemy, to go there. This vision has increased my love for all people. I will soon be writing my experience of prayer, fasting, and my trips to Heaven and Hell. As we turn to the Word of God, we can understand some foundational truths that are important as we consider praying for the lost throughout the world. The Bible makes it very clear that God's desire is to see all saved from perishing—so much so that He gave His beloved Son to make a way where there was no way.

Second Peter 3:9 (AMPC) says, "The Lord does not delay and is not tardy or slow about what He promises, according to some people's conception of slowness, but He is long-suffering (extraordinarily patient) toward you, not desiring that any should perish, but that all should turn to repentance."

"And He (that same Jesus Himself) is the propitiation (the atoning sacrifice) for our sins, and not for ours alone but also for (the sins of) the whole world" (1 John 2:2 AMPC).

"For God so loved the world that He gave His only begotten Son, that whoever believes in Him should not perish but have everlasting life. For God did not send the Son into the world to condemn the world, but that the world through Him might be saved" (John 3:16–17 NASB).

God's will is that all men should be saved. When we pray for the lost, we are praying in accordance with God's will for them. God has also called us to love one another. Someone has said that prayer is "love on its knees." As we pray for those whom God loves, He fills us with compassion and love for them. Certainly it was God's love for mankind that brought Jesus to the cross. Only eternity will reveal the incredible numbers of souls that have been saved through the tears shed as people prayed. Indeed, love is our greatest asset in the saving of souls. We pray because the lost will not, and indeed, cannot be saved unless someone prays for them. This is a shocking statement that sounds unbelievable until we view the Biblical portrayal of the lost:

"But now you seek to kill Me, a Man who has told you the truth which I heard from God. Abraham did not do this. You do the deeds of your father." Then they said to Him, 'We were not born of fornication; we have one Father—God.' Jesus said to them, 'If God were your Father, you would love Me, for I proceeded forth and came from God; nor have I come of Myself, but He sent Me. Why do you not understand My speech? Because you are not able to listen to My word. You are of your father the devil, and the desires of your father you want to do. He was a murderer from the beginning, and does not stand in the truth, because there is no truth in him. When he speaks a lie, he speaks from his own resources, for he is a liar and the father of it. But because I tell the truth, you do not believe Me'" (John 8:40–45 NKJV). *Lost people are the children of Satan.*

"So I said, 'Who are You, Lord?' And He said, 'I am Jesus, whom you are persecuting. But rise and stand on your feet; for I have appeared to you for this purpose, to make you a minister and a witness both of the things which you have seen and of the things which I will yet reveal to you. I will deliver you from the Jewish people, as well as from the Gentiles, to whom I now send you, to open their eyes, in order to turn them from darkness to light, and from the power of Satan to God, that they may receive forgiveness of sins and an inheritance among those who are sanctified by faith in Me'" (Acts 26:15–18 NKJV). *Lost people are under the power of Satan.*

"But no one can enter the strong man's house and plunder his property unless he first binds the strong man, and then he will plunder his house" (Mark 3:27 NASB). *Lost people are bound by the strong man (prisoners).*

"But even if our gospel is veiled, it is veiled to those who are perishing, whose minds the god of this age has blinded, who do not believe, lest the light of the gospel of the glory of Christ, who is the image of God, should shine on them" (2 Corinthians 4:3–4 NKJV). *Lost people are blinded by Satan.*

Lewis Sperry Chafer says, "The blinding or veiling of the mind" mentioned in 2 Corinthians 4:3–4 (NKJV) causes a universal incapacity to comprehend the way of salvation and is imposed upon unregenerate man by the arch enemy of God in his attempts to hinder the purpose of God in redemption. It is a condition of mind against which man can have no power."

"Wherein in time past ye walked according to the course of this world, according to the prince of the power of the air, the spirit that now worketh in the children of disobedience" (Ephesians 2:2 KJV).

"We know that we are of God, and that the whole world lies in the power of the evil one" (1 John 5:19 NASB).

Ephesians 2:2 (KJV) talks about the "spirit that now worketh." The Greek word for worketh is *energeo*, which means to energize. We learn from this that the lost are literally energized by the spirit of the devil. The lost person does not have understanding about this, does not realize that he/she is in bondage because he/she believes that he/she is free. But, in truth, his/her every action is dictated by the prince of the air. As we read John 5:19, we know that we are of God, and the whole world lies in wickedness. This means that the whole world lies prostrate under the influence of the devil. Webster's Dictionary defines prostrate as "to lie with face downward in abject submission, to be completely subjugated." This definition, together with the reference from 1 John, helps us to see that the lost person is not trying to be free, but is quietly lying under the power of Satan.

I believe Mark 3:27 is the most important verse in the Bible concerning winning the lost to Jesus Christ. When you read this verse, what does it mean to you? The way I understand it, no lost person will be saved unless someone frees him or her. We must engage in spiritual warfare. We must use the weapons of warfare, which God has given us to win the war against Satan.

One of the greatest preachers of all times was Charles H. Spurgeon, who said:

> I confess that I had been tutored in piety, put into my cradle by prayerful hands and lulled to sleep by songs about Jesus. I had heard the gospel continually, yet when the Word of the Lord came to me with power, it was as new as if I had lived among the tribes of Central Africa and had never heard the tidings of the cleansing fountain filled with blood, drawn from the Savior's veins.
>
> When for the first time I received the Gospel and my soul was saved, I thought that I had never really heard it before. I began to think that preacher to whom I had listened had not truly preached it. But on looking back, I am inclined to believe that I had heard the Gospel fully preached many hundreds of times before. This was the difference: I then heard it as though I did not hear it. When I did hear it, the message may not have been any clearer in itself than it had been at former times, but the power of the Holy Spirit was present to open my ears and to guide the message to my heart.
>
> Then I thought I had never heard the truth preached before. Now I am persuaded that the light shone often on my eyes, but I was blind. Therefore, I thought that

the light had never come there. The light was shining all the while, but there was no power to receive it. The eyeball of the soul was not sensitive to the divine beams. (*My Conversion*, Springdale: Whitaker, 1996, 26–28)

As you read the words of Spurgeon, you might realize that sharing the Gospel with those for whom no one has prayed is like asking a blind man to see the sunlight the same way you do. It is not possible. He cannot see because he is blind.

It is the Holy Spirit who removes the demonic blinders and opens the mind and heart to the Gospel. The Gospel message is foolishness to the lost person (1Corinthians 2:14). It is foolishness because he is in the strong man's house. This is the reason he is not receptive to the Gospel. The word foolishness in the Greek is *moria*, from which the word moron is derived. Webster's defines "moron" as, "the highest classification of mental deficiency, above imbecile and idiot."

When you are trying to share the Gospel with someone for whom you have not prayed—I mean really, really prayed—you can do more harm than good. We need to understand that this person is in a prison. He is guarded by demonic forces. Sharing the Gospel with anyone is a step into a spiritual war zone. It is essential that we have an understanding of spiritual warfare and weaponry. If we are going to enter the strong man's house, we must be fully equipped with the weapons and protection that God provides for us.

It is so important that we be in a state of personal readiness in order to be effective in our prayers for the lost. When we are praying, we are doing combat! We fight by praying. We take ground by praying. When we are praying, the devil is losing because he has no defense against prayer. I have traveled to forty-six states throughout the country in the last sixteen years, preaching and teaching in more than one thousand churches, many Bible colleges and universities. I have discovered that many people (Christians) have not even heard about spiritual warfare. Many are not even willing to believe that there is a devil! My response to that is simple. *Please read your Bible.* You will find out that Satan is real and that there is a very real need for being prepared. The Word of

God gives us guidelines for personal spiritual readiness. And God has provided the weapons we need to enter into the battle.

Righteousness and Faith

The imputed righteousness of Christ, which comes through His shed blood, is what gives us boldness to come before the throne of His grace. It is absolutely indispensable for effective prayer. Personal righteousness is also crucial.

"If I regard iniquity in my heart, the Lord will not hear me" (Psalm 66:18 KJV).

"If you remain in me and my words remain in you, ask whatever you want, and it will be done for you" (John 15:7 NET).

Check Your Attitude

As we approach the Lord in prayer, we must be aware of the attitude we have as we come. Here are some of the characteristics of an attitude that is pleasing to God:

"Return and tell Hezekiah the leader of My people, 'Thus says the Lord, the God of David your father: "I have heard your prayer, I have seen your tears; surely I will heal you. On the third day you shall go up to the house of the Lord"'" (2 Kings 20:5 NKJV).

King Hezekiah was very real with God, as he received the prophetic word that he would soon die. He was not afraid or ashamed to turn his face to the wall and let the tears flow.

"Those who sow in tears shall reap in joy. He who continually goes forth weeping, bearing seed for sowing, shall doubtless come again with rejoicing, bringing his sheaves with him" (Psalm 126:5–6 NKJV).

Farmers are humble people, knowing that planting time and harvest are both seasons of hard work—and sometimes tears. They must go out to plant, prepared, carrying the seed for owing. There will be much sweat pouring from their brows, muscles aching, and tears flowing.

But at harvest time, they rejoice as they bring in the harvest, the fruits of their labor.

> And standing behind Him at his feet, weeping she began to wet His feet with her tears, and kept wiping them with the hair of her head, and kissing His feet and anointing them with the perfume. Now when the Pharisee who had invited Him saw this, he said to himself, "If this man were a prophet, he would know who and what sort of person this woman is who is touching him, that she is a sinner." And Jesus answered him, "Simon I have something to say to you." And he replied, "Say it, Teacher." Then Jesus told him this story: "A moneylender had two debtors: one owed five hundred denarii, and the other fifty. When they were unable to repay, he graciously forgave them both. So which of them will love him more? Simon answered and said, "I suppose the one whom he forgave more." And he said to him, "You have judged correctly." Turning toward the woman, He said to Simon, "Do you see this woman? I entered your house; you gave Me no water for My feet, but she has wet My feet with her tears and wiped them with her hair. You gave Me no kiss, but she, since the time I came in, has not ceased to kiss My feet. You did not anoint My head with oil, but she anointed My feet with perfume. For this reason I say to you, her sins, which are many, have been forgiven, for she loved much; but he who is forgiven little, loves little." Then He said to her, "Your sins have been forgiven." Those who were reclining at the table with Him began to say to themselves, "Who is this man who even forgives sins?" And he said to the woman, "Your faith has saved you; go in peace." (Luke 7:38–50 NASB)

What a beautiful picture of an "attitude of gratitude." When we go to the Lord in prayer, we bring our petitions, making known our requests to Him. But, when we approach Him with thanksgiving, remembering all that He has already done in response to our prayers—tears may flow. There will also be an increased attitude of expectancy.

"Who in the days of his flesh, when he had offered up prayers and supplications with strong crying and tears unto him that was able to save him from death, and was heard in that he feared; Though he were a Son, yet learned he obedience by the things which he suffered" (Hebrews 5:7–8 KJV).

Jesus, our Savior and Lord, cried out to His Father, letting the tears flow. Note that this passage says that God hears His prayers *because* of His deep reverence for God. An attitude of reverence and awe for the One to whom we pray is an important key.

Blood of Jesus

We then must remember that the blood of Jesus Christ is one of the most powerful weapons we have. "And they overcame him by the blood of the Lamb and by the word of their testimony, and they loved not their lives unto the death." When you are going to pray for the lost, you need to know how you can use this powerful weapon, the blood of Jesus Christ. The blood of Jesus Christ has positive and negative effects—positive for believers in Him and negative for the devil and his demons" (Revelation 12:11 KJV).

"And they shall take some of the blood and put it on the two doorposts and on the lintel of the houses where they eat it. And you shall take a bunch of hyssop, dip it in the blood that is in the basin, and strike the lintel and the two doorposts with the blood that is in the basin. And none of you shall go out of the door of his house until morning. For the LORD will pass through to strike the Egyptians; and when He sees the blood on the lintel and on the two doorposts, the LORD will pass over the door and not allow the destroyer to come into your houses to strike you" (Exodus 12:7, 22–23 NKJV).

God instructed Moses to have the Israelites apply the blood of the lamb on the doorposts and lintels of their houses. Those who lived in the houses with the blood on the doorposts and lintels were protected. In all the other homes, the firstborn (human and livestock) all died.

As you begin to pray for the lost person, please ask the Lord to cover you, your family, and your possessions with His blood. Why do you need to be covered with the blood of Jesus Christ? When you enter into spiritual warfare, beginning to fight against Satan, he is going to retaliate. We do not need to fear, but please do not leave anything uncovered. When every person and everything is covered with the blood of Jesus, we have total protection against Satan.

I remember one time while we were still living in Pakistan, I was invited to pray for a family. This family had been affected by demons and the devil. Their livestock were dying because of the demonic attack. Some magic charms had been placed under the manger by some witch doctors. Because of these magic charms, the animals were dying. I arrived at their home about midnight. There was no electricity, so it was totally dark, other than a candle or kerosene lamp. As I began to pray, I felt as if someone was choking me. All of a sudden, I began to apply the blood of Jesus over my throat. As I was doing this, the choking stopped, but I continued to apply the blood of Jesus. As I repeated over and over, "the blood of Jesus, the blood of Jesus," I heard a loud noise and found out that the power of the demons over the household and over the livestock had been destroyed. They were free. Praise the Lord! There is power in the blood of Jesus.

Another time when we were living in South Africa, a family brought their daughter into the church. She was possessed by demons. I was just a visiting pastor, and it was my duty to be there. The senior pastor and other staff pastors began to pray for the girl. They were asking the demons to leave, but the demons were refusing to leave. The senior pastor then asked me to join them in praying for the girl. The Lord put in my heart that I should be applying the blood of Jesus against the demons. As I started to apply the blood of Jesus, the demons began to scream and were saying, "We are burning; we are burning." After a short while, the demons were gone, and the girl was free. She accepted

Jesus Christ as her Lord and Savior. Praise the Lord for the power of the blood of Jesus!

"Therefore, since the children share in flesh and blood, He Himself likewise also partook of the same, that through death He might render powerless him who had the power of death, that is, the devil" (Hebrews 2:14 NASB).

Through Jesus's shed blood, His death on the cross, He destroyed the power that Satan had. *Strong's Dictionary* defines destroy as to render entirely useless, to make void. When Jesus went to the cross, all the claims, and all the authority which the devil had stolen from Adam on this earth, were totally cancelled. Because of the blood of Jesus, Satan absolutely has no claim, no right at all over anyone or anything. All the power the devil is using against people is just a deception or a bluff. When we apply the blood of Jesus Christ, we are remembering that Satan and all his demons were defeated at the cross. All his power and authority were destroyed.

Armor of God

"Finally, my brethren, be strong in the Lord and in the power of His might. Put on the whole armor of God, that you may be able to stand against the wiles of the devil. For we do not wrestle against flesh and blood, but against principalities, against powers, against the rulers of the darkness of this age, against spiritual hosts of wickedness in the heavenly places. Therefore take up the whole armor of God, that you may be able to withstand in the evil day, and having done all, to stand. Stand therefore, having girded your waist with truth, having put on the breastplate of righteousness, and having shod your feet with the preparation of the gospel of peace; above all, taking the shield of faith with which you will be able to quench all the fiery darts of the wicked one. And take the helmet of salvation, and the sword of the Spirit, which is the word of God" (Ephesians 6:10–17 NKJV).

The word of God says, "And ye shall know the truth, and the truth shall make you free" (John 8:32 KJV). The belt of truth is where we hang all of the weapons. As Christian soldiers, we must have the belt of truth around our waists, just as soldiers serving in the military have a belt for their weapons. The belt of truth not only holds our weapons (for easy access), it also protects us from nakedness, so that we will not be found naked (unprepared) before God and the world. Peter said, "Gird your mind with the truth." The belt was also used by the Roman soldiers to tuck in their toga, the loose, flowing garment that they wore. By tucking it under the belt, they had freer movement and were able to run faster.

"Even the righteousness of God through faith in Jesus Christ for all those who believe" (Romans 3:22 NASB).

"Abraham believed God, and it was credited to him as righteousness" (Romans 4:3 NASB).

In Ephesians 6, we are instructed to put on the breastplate of righteousness. It is not our own righteousness. As Romans 3:22 tells us, the righteousness from God—the righteousness that will adequately be part of our spiritual weaponry—comes through our faith in Jesus Christ.

You are also instructed to "shod your feet with the preparation of the gospel of peace" or to "have your feet fitted with the readiness that comes from the gospel of peace." If you were being called into battle in the natural, you would put on heavy boots with high tops and maybe even steel toes. The purpose of the boots would be to protect your feet against uneven terrain, allowing you to move more quickly and efficiently, providing greater stability as you carry the load of your other weapons. Romans 10:15b (NASB) says, "As it is written, 'How beautiful are the feet of those who bring good news!'" Our feet need to be shod so that we can move quickly and at the same time stand fast!

Then we are to take up the shield of faith. Psalm 3:3 (KJV) says, "But thou, O Lord, art a shield for me; my glory, and the lifter up of mine head." And Psalm 33:20 (NKJV) reminds us again, "He is our help and our shield." Ephesians 6 tells us that with the shield of faith, we will be able to quench all the fiery darts of the wicked one. When we intimately know our Father God (because we have obeyed Jesus's words in Matthew 6:33 (KJV): "Seek ye first the kingdom of God and

His righteousness," then we have faith in Him as our protector and our provider—the shield about us. It is also important to remember that as we link our shield with the shields of our brothers and sisters in Christ, we create a powerfully strong wall barring the enemy from advancing his cause.

We must also protect our heads, so we are told to put on the helmet of salvation. Isaiah 59:17 (KJV) reads, "For he put on righteousness as a breastplate, and a helmet of salvation (Yeshua) upon his head." Jesus's name in Hebrew is Yeshua. Yeshua means salvation. Salvation is Jesus Christ. When we put on the helmet of salvation, we are "putting on" Jesus! And when we put on the helmet of salvation, we are protecting our minds.

Thus far, the belt of Truth, the breastplate of righteousness, feet fitted with the readiness that comes from the gospel of peace, the shield of faith, and the helmet of salvation—all are vital parts of the armor. Most of the time, we are told that all of these are defensive/protective in nature. But the Lord has showed me that all of the parts of the armor of God are defensive—yes—but also offensive. These will not only protect you, but you can also fight with them. For example, the shoes—Jesus said to go trample the scorpions. "Behold, I have given you authority to tread on serpents and **scorpions**, and over all the power of the enemy, and nothing will injure you" (Luke 10:19 NASB). The shield of faith does quench the fiery darts, but you can also hit your enemy with the shield.

Finally, we are instructed to take up the sword of the Spirit, which is the Word of God. Hebrews 4:12 (NKJV) says, "For the Word of God is living and powerful, and sharper than any two-edged sword, piercing even to the division of soul and spirit, and of joints and marrow, and is a discerner of thoughts and intents of the heart."

Biblical commentator Matthew Henry wrote: "To the Christian armed for defense in battle, the apostle recommends only one weapon of attack; but it is enough, the sword of the Spirit, which is the word of God. It subdues and mortifies evil desires and blasphemous thoughts as they rise within; and answers unbelief and error as they assault from without. A single text, well understood, and rightly applied, at once destroys a temptation or an objection, and subdues the most formidable adversary."

Jesus modeled responding to Satan's temptations in Matthew 4:1–11(NASB):

> Then Jesus was led up by the Spirit into the wilderness to be tempted by the devil. And after He had fasted forty days and forty nights, He then became hungry. And the tempter came and said to Him, "If You are the Son of God, command that these stones become bread." But He answered and said, "It is written, 'Man shall not live on bread alone, but on every word that proceeds out of the mouth of God.'" Then the devil took Him into the holy city and had Him stand on the pinnacle of the temple, and said to Him, "If You are the Son of God, throw Yourself down; for it is written, 'He will command His angels concerning you' and 'On their hands they will bear you up, so that you will not strike your foot against a stone.'" Jesus said to him, "On the other hand, it is written, 'You shall not put the Lord your God to the test.'" Again, the devil took Him to a very high mountain and showed Him all the kingdoms of the world and their glory; and he said to Him, "All these things I will give You, if You fall down and worship me.' Then Jesus said to him, "Go, Satan! For it is written, 'You shall worship the Lord your God, and serve Him only.'" Then the devil left Him; and behold, angels came and began to minister to Him.

The apostles gave themselves to prayer and the ministry of the Word because they had learned the vital need for prayer and the amazing power of the Word.

"Rejoice always, **pray without ceasing**, in everything give thanks; for this is the will of God in Christ Jesus for you" (1 Thessalonians 5:17 NKJV).

"We will give ourselves continually to prayer and to the ministry of the Word" (Acts 6:4 NKJV).

God gave His only Son for the entire world, but only those who believe in Him will be benefited. Jesus willingly went to the cross, in our place and in the place of all those who are still lost. We must learn how to pray effectively for those who do not yet know Him. Charles G. Finney said, "In the case of an important friend, the very condition on which he is to be saved from hell may be the fervency and importunity of your prayer for that individual." (*Revivals of Religion*, Old Tappan: Revell, n.d.; *Charles G. Finney: An Autobiography*, Westwood: Revell, 1876.)

Prayer is a powerful tool. James 5:16b (NKJV) says, "The effectual fervent prayer of a righteous man availeth much." When the atomic bombs were dropped on Japan during World War II, some ninety-two thousand people were killed. We read in the Bible that when Assyria besieged Jerusalem, King Hezekiah prayed for God's protection. God sent an angel that night and killed 185,000 Assyrian soldiers. Hezekiah's prayer was twice as explosive as the atomic bomb! In this account, we see prayer is strong enough to destroy enemies. How much more certain is its power to save souls?

"And He saw that there was no man, And was astonished that there was no one to intercede; Then His own arm brought salvation to Him, And His righteousness upheld Him" (Isaiah 59:16 NASB).

God was astonished that there was not a single intercessor for Israel. As Andrew Murray commented on God's seeking for an intercessor, "He often had to wonder and complain that there was no intercessor, no one to stir himself up to take hold of His strength. And He still waits and wonders in our day that there are not more intercessors; that all His children do not give themselves to this highest and holiest work; that many of those who do so do not engage in it more intensely and perseveringly. He wonders to find ministers of His Gospel complaining that their duties do not allow them to find time for that which He counts their first, their highest, their most delightful, their alone effective work."

"First of all, then, I urge that entreaties and prayers, petitions, and thanksgivings be made on behalf of all men, For kings and all who are in authority, so we may lead a tranquil life in all godliness and dignity. This is good and acceptable in the sight of God our Savior, Who desires all men to be saved and to come to the knowledge of the truth" (1 Timothy 2:1–4 NASB).

In the above passage from 1 Timothy, it is very clear that God's number one priority for us is to pray for others. Please hear the cry of God's heart as He calls on us to pray. Often, as Christians we think that God has called us first to preach the gospel. I believe that preaching the gospel is actually second. First, we must pray for the lost souls. You can preach without love, but prayer will need your deepest and strongest love for the lost person. And, as you pray for the lost person, your love for him or her grows.

Model Prayer for the Lost

My dearest Heavenly Father, I come to you in the name of your son Jesus Christ and through his holy and precious blood, which was shed for our salvation. Dear Heavenly Father, your Word says that you do not want anyone to perish, but you want everyone to be saved. It is also written in your Word in John 3:16 (KJV) and Luke 19:10 (KJV), "For God so loved the world, that he gave his only begotten Son, that whosoever believeth in him should not perish, but have everlasting life." "For the Son of man is come to seek and to save that which was lost."

Lord Jesus, it is written in your Word, in 2 Corinthians 10:4–5 (KJV), "For the weapons of our warfare are not carnal, but mighty through God to the pulling down of strong holds; Casting down imaginations, and every high thing that exalteth itself against the knowledge of God, and bringing into captivity every thought to the obedience of Christ;" Lord Jesus, I thank you for the authority that you have given to me. You said in Luke 10:19 (KJV), "Behold, I give unto you Power to tread on serpents and scorpions, and over all the Power of the enemy: and nothing shall by any means hurt you." I take authority in the name of Jesus Christ, according to His word and by the power of His Blood; every imagination and thought which is exalting against God's word, I demolish them, and I bring them into the total submission and obedience of Lord Jesus Christ. I also command the prince of the power of the air to leave these lost people, and that the blindfolds from their eyes would be removed in the name of Jesus Christ.

As it is written in 2 Corinthians 4:3–4 (KJV): "But if our gospel be hid, it is hid to them that are lost: In whom the god of this world hath blinded the minds of them which believe not, lest the light of the glorious gospel of Christ, who is the image of God, should shine unto them." I also bind the strong man/strong men who is/are controlling these lost people, and I command them to leave these people right now in the mighty and powerful name of Jesus Christ. As it is written in the Gospel of Matthew and Mark, Jesus says in Matthew 12:29 (KJV), "Or else how can one enter into a strong man's house, and spoil his goods, except he first bind the strong man? And then he will spoil his house." And in Mark 3:27 (KJV): "No man can enter into a strong man's house, and spoil his goods, except he will first bind the strong man; and then he will spoil his house."

I pray to you, my dear Heavenly Father, please send your Holy Spirit in the name of Jesus Christ to convict these people of their sins, righteousness of God, and the judgment of God as it is written in John 16:8 (KJV): "And when he is come, he will reprove the world of sin, and of righteousness, and of judgment." Please send Your holy angels to block their way toward sin because Your word says in Hebrews 1:14 (KJV), "Are they not all ministering spirits, sent forth to minister for them who shall be heirs of salvation?" Let these people be led to Christ Jesus and let their eyes be open to receive Jesus as their personal savior, because according to Acts 4:12 (KJV), "Neither is there salvation in any other: for there is none other name under heaven given among men, whereby we must be saved," but by the name of Jesus Christ. I pray this in the name of Jesus Christ, the Son of the Most High God. Amen.

CHAPTER 39

Stand Strong

When I came to the United States, the Lord showed me a vision of the American church. It is full of goats—"I'm going to bring persecution to the church, to separate the goats from the sheep" (Matthew 25:31–46). So it is very, very important for us to be prepared for that time, that when it comes, we will not be lost. We will not give up. We should not shrink back, but rather stay strong. We should be willing to say, "Yes Lord Jesus. Even if I have to die, I'm willing to die." I believe that the Lord brought my family here to the United States to help equip people for the persecution that is coming. He has called us to share the Truth of His Gospel and to share the truth about Islam. He is calling you to seek Truth and to spend time in His Word every day.

Remember the story of Shadrach, Meshach, and Abed-Nego, or Daniel in the lion's den? Jehovah God worked in miraculous ways in the lives of those who would not deny Him. And, though Saul was an influential leader responsible for persecuting followers of Jesus, the Lord Himself met him on the road to Damascus. Saul was so transformed when he encountered the Truth, which is Jesus (Jesus said, "I am the Way and the Truth and the Life (John 14:6 KJV), that he changed his name to Paul. Jehovah God is still doing amazing miracles today. And He is faithful! Hallelujah!

Sixteen years ago, when the Lord Jesus Christ brought us to this wonderful and beautiful country, my wife and I were praying and asking God, "Lord, please show us your plan for us in the United States."

When we lived in Pakistan, I was the pastor of four churches, and was also overseeing another ten churches. After arriving in the United States, we were still asking the Lord for clarity. As we were praying and seeking His guidance, He gave me this passage from the Bible:

"And when they had preached the gospel to that city, and had taught many, they returned again to Lystra, and to Iconium, and Antioch, Confirming the souls of the disciples, and exhorting them to continue in the faith, and that we must through much tribulation enter into the kingdom of God" (Acts 14:21–22 KJV).

The Lord made it clear that He wanted me to encourage the people of the United States to stand strong and to be true to the faith. That is so very, very important. Jehovah God has also called us to "Remember those who are in prison as if you were in prison with them. Remember those who are mistreated as if you were suffering with them" (Hebrews 13:3 EXB). My family and I have experienced persecution firsthand.

I want to encourage you to stay strong in your faith. The God we serve is faithful. We can do mighty things for Him, just like Shadrach, Meshach, and Abed-Nego, and just like Daniel. The God we serve is able to rescue us if we are faithful and we worship Him only—not the golden images all around us. In Acts 4:12 (NKJV) it is written, "Nor is there salvation in any other, for there is no other name under heaven given among men by which we must be saved."

Whenever you find yourself doubting how far you can go, just remember how far you have come. Remember everything you have faced, all the battles you have won, and all the fears you have overcome. He is calling you, my son and my daughter, and saying, "Do not fear, for I am with you. I will not leave you nor forsake you. I will carry you through in my arms. I will be with you always."

We are more than conquerors through Christ Jesus. Remember greater is He who is in you than he who is in the World. You are a mighty winner. Don't ever give up. You are only a few inches away from your victory.

God bless you, my dear brothers and sisters. As we stay strong for Jesus, He will stay strong for us. The only way that you can stay strong in your faith is when you are on your knees. It is very difficult to fall when you are on your knees. Once you get down on your knees, God will stand up for you. When God stands up for you, no one can stand against you. Remember the story of Stephen? When he was stoned, Stephen saw something amazing. Jesus was standing at the right hand of the Father. We read that Jesus is seated at the right hand of the Father, but Stephen saw Him "standing at the right hand of God" (Acts 7:55 NKJV).

This is a powerful reminder that if we will stand for Jesus, He will stand for us. He is waiting with open arms, and His welcoming voice is saying, "Welcome, my son, welcome, my daughter." Through His shed blood, we can be free. We can *know* the promise of eternal life. We can rejoice as we hear His voice say, "It is done!"

APPENDICES

When Homes Were Burning

APPENDIX 1

Concept of Sin in Christianity and Islam

Growing up in Pakistan, we used to believe that there are three true religions in the world, Judaism, Christianity, and Islam because they all worship the same god and only one god. This is the belief of many people. They think that all religions teach the same set of moral values with only minor variations.

Factual understanding of the major doctrines of Jesus and Allah/ Muhammad reveal superficial similarities but also that the teachings are often very different. As a result, the actions that stem from these beliefs are also different.

The Source of Sin

In Islam, the origin of sin is Allah. Islam claims that humans were created in a state of equilibrium: sinless at birth (Sura 16:78; Pickthall 30:30 and 98:5) and with pure Islamic faith (Bukhari Vol. 8, Hadith No. 597). The Qur'an makes it perfectly clear that no person is really free to choose good or evil; Allah leads people astray.

Sura 7:178, "Whomsoever Allâh guides, he is the guided one, and whomsoever He sends astray, those! They are the losers." (see also Sura 7:179; 13:31; 95:4–5; 4:142; 39:57).

Thus, in Islam, Adam did not bring sin into the world. Indeed Allah had destined Adam to sin—forty years before he created him (Bukhari Vol. 8, Hadith No. 611; see also Sura 9:51).

In Christianity, humans are believed to be born sinners; by virtue of Adam's sin, we inherit a sinful nature (Romans 5:12), and so people commit sin because they are sinners.

Definition of Sin

In Islam, sin is sometimes intention of heart (except unbelief) (Sura 33:5; Bukhari Vol. 1, Hadith No. 1; 2:284); but other times it is only wrong actions (Bukhari Vol 8, Hadith 498). The Qur'an recognizes that all living persons are inherently good, and it is their actions and devotion to Allah that enables them to obtain salvation. Even demons are capable of regaining salvation (Ibn Kathir on 55:71).

In Christianity, sin includes actions, but is primarily wrong thoughts, desires, and inclinations, a rebellious defiance of God (Exodus 20:17, Matthew 5:28, Romans 1:21, 1 John 2:15), as these are the source of your actions (Matthew 12:34, Luke 6:45).

The Seriousness of Sin

In Christianity, there is no changing standard regarding sin: the standard is always God's holiness. Be holy for I am Holy (Leviticus 11:45, 19:2; 1 Peter 1:16); I the Lord do not change (Malachi 3:6, Hebrews 13:8); and all have sinned and fall short of the glory of God (Romans 3:23). For example, adultery is completely forbidden (Matthew 5:27–28), whereas in Islam, limited prostitution is permitted (Sura 24:33, 4:24, 33:37). Unlike Christianity, Islam does not consider all sin equally wrong. Sins are divided into different categories, but are most usefully separated into greater and lesser sins. There are several lists of great sins (albeit conflicting), which can be summarized as:

1. To join partners in worship with Allah

2. To practice sorcery
3. Murder without just (legal) cause
4. To charge usury (money lent at high interest)
5. To consume the property of an orphan
6. To be a coward in battle
7. To be undutiful to one's parents
8. To give a false witness (lying)
9. To kill your child lest he should share your food with you (i.e., poverty)
10. To commit illegal sexual intercourse with the wife of your neighbor (a.k.a., adultery)
11. Alcohol
12. Gambling

Even though these are listed as great sins, they are obviously not seen as very serious according to Muhammad's teachings. As seen above, though adultery is forbidden, prostitution (Sura 24:33) and limited (temporary) marriage are permissible (Sura 4:24). Thus, in Islam, the seriousness, and even the definition, of sin varies. For example, alcohol is forbidden on earth (Sura 5:90–91) but in Islamic paradise, alcohol is allowed (Sura 56:18; 76:5, 17; 78:34). On earth, Islam forbids more than four wives (excepting temporary wives, and concubines) and adultery (Sura 4:3), but in Islamic paradise, seventy-two virgins (at-Tirmidhi, Hadith No. 1067, 1494 [Alim Software]; see Sura 56:22–40; Ibn Kathir on 55:72) and boys (Sura 52:24, 56:17, 76:19). Lying is generally forbidden, but the doctrine of Al-Taqiyya [legal right of Muslims to deceive non-Muslims] permits lying. Muhammad believed that lying was acceptable and said, "Allah willing, if ever I take an oath to do something, and later on I find that it is more beneficial to do something different, I will do the thing which is better, and give expiation for my oath." (Bukhari, Vol. 4, Hadith No. 361).

Allah had taught in the Qur'an that Muslims are not bound by their oaths (Sura 66:2). Lying is permitted because Allah can deceive. In fact, Allah calls himself the greatest of deceivers [Allaahu Khayrul-maakiriin], (Sura 3:54, 8:30) and leads people astray (Sura 4:88, 143;

7:178,186; 13:27, etc). Murder, even though it is a great sin, is actually commanded to prevent or remove *al- Fitnah* [opposition (Sura 2:191 and 2:217) or disbelief (Sura 8:39)]. Muslims are even commanded to slay unbelievers if they do not convert (Sura 9:5, etc.). Thus, the great sin of murder is commanded if unbelievers do not convert or when *Al Fitnah* exists. No Muslim should be put to death for murdering an unbeliever (Bukhari Vol. 4, Hadith No. 283). Muhammad permitted sorcery although it is listed as a great sin (Muslim, Book 26, Hadith No. 5449, 5452, 5456). In keeping with this attitude to the great sins, Muhammad forbade children from obeying or even being near their parents, if their parents were unbelievers (Sura 9:23). Despite all these irregularities, Allah sought to emphasize the necessity of sin when his messenger said: "By Him in Whose Hand is my life, if you were not to commit sin, Allah would sweep you out of existence and He would replace (you by) those people who would commit sin and seek forgiveness from Allah, and He would have pardoned them" (Muslim, Vol. 4, Book, 37, Hadith No. 6622, 6621). This shows how serious Allah regards sin. If you do not sin, Allah will wipe you out and replace you with people who will sin. It is then incumbent upon Muslims to sin, so that they will repent and seek Allah. How then, can Muslims get into heaven? Allah weighs their sins and good deeds in a balance (Sura 7:8, 9; 21:47; 23:101–3). If the good deeds outweigh the bad deeds, then entry is assured ... To aid a Muslim in this venture, Allah proclaims, "Those who avoid great sins (see Sura 4:31) ... except the small sins, verily, your Lord is of vast forgiveness" (Sura 53:32). Good deeds remove sinful deeds (Sura 5:39; 11:114; Bukhari Vol. 1, Hadith No. 504). Punishment now, means no punishment after death (Bukhari, Vol. 1, Hadith No. 17). Additionally, every letter of the Qur'an that is read in Arabic accredits the reader with ten good deeds recorded (at-Tirmidhi, Hadith No. 318 [Alim Software] and others). Good deeds can be multiplied many times, up to seven hundred times (Sura 4:40, 6:160; Bukhari Vo. 1. Hadith No. 40) and are easily obtained (Bukhari Vol. 4, Hadith No. 112, 514; Vol. 8, Hadith No. 335, 412; No. 9, Hadith No. 507). Reciting the confession of faith is recorded as ten good deeds (at-Tirmidhi, Hadith No. 308 [Alim Software]). All this gives the impression that sin is easily forgiven and seems to convey the certainty of entry into heaven. However Muhammad, under Allah's inspiration, revealed that good deeds will never get you into heaven (Bukhari, Vol. 7, Hadith No. 577, and Vol. 8, Hadith No. 474) for Allah may not forgive you (Sura 4:116). The last Rightly Guided Caliph said, "I swear to Allah that I do not feel safe from Allah's cunning (deceit) even if one of my feet is already in Paradise." (Khalid Muhammad Khalid, *Successors of the Apostle*, p. 114, quoted by Anwar al-Jundi, *Mizan al-Islam*, p. 170).

Summary

As we have seen, sin is not a serious issue in Islam, and even great sins are forgiven easily. Christianity, however, never changes the standard, and forgiveness is never obtained by doing good works. It is the heart and mind that needs to be changed. In Christianity, forgiveness of sin is only available through the atoning death of Jesus Christ (Islam forbids atonement, Sura 4:112; and see 17:15, etc). The God of the Bible and the God of Islam too often have different standards regarding holiness; Allah has an arbitrary standard and requires Muslims to sin; Yahweh (Jehovah) requires perfection of heart, mind, soul, and body (Matthew 5:48)—they can never be contaminated by sin and still enter heaven without atonement by the blood of Lord Jesus. Only faith in the righteousness of Christ offers forgiveness now and a certain hope of heaven.

Allah claims thirty times in the Qur'an that he misleads/sends astray people and that he is the greatest deceiver [Allaahu Khayrul-maakiriin] (Sura 3:54, 8:30). Allah says that he leads people astray (Sura 4:88, 143; 6:39, 126; 7:178,186; 9:51; 13:27, 31; 14:4; 16:93; 17:13, 97; 30:29; 35:8; 36:8–10; 39:23; 40:33, 34, 74; 42:44, 46; 74:31). Even the first Rightly Guided Caliph said, "I swear to Allah that I do not feel safe from Allah's cunning even if one of my feet is already inside paradise." (Khalid Muhammad Khalid, *Successors of the Apostle*, p. 114, quoted by Anwar al-Jundi, *Mizan al-Islam*, p. 170). Muhammad believed that lying was acceptable and even taught how to expiate [make amends for] an oath, "Allah willing, if ever I take an oath to do something, and later on I find that it is more beneficial to do something different, I will do the thing which is better, and give expiation for my oath." (Bukhari, Vol. 4, Hadith No. 361) Muhammad saw nothing wrong in practicing duplicity. It was his common practice to say one thing and do exactly the opposite if something appealed to him otherwise. He sent men to kill people unawares in their homes and also gave them permission to tell lies in order to deceive the people being killed. (A. Guillaume, *The Life of Muhammad*; Bukhari, Vol. 4, Hadith No. 143).

Imam Jafar Sadiq said, "You belong to a religion that whosoever conceals it, Allah will honour him and whosoever reveals it, Allah will disgrace and humiliate him." (Ahmad Abdullah Salamah, *The Sunni and Shia Perspective of The Holy Qur'an*). This is called al-Taqiyya [legal deception]. Sura 3:28 and others record that Muslims cannot take unbelievers for real friends (else they will cease to be true Muslims), "Let not the believers take the disbelievers as Auliya^ (supporters, helpers, etc.) instead of the believers, and whoever does that will never be helped by Allah in any way, except if you indeed fear a danger from them. And Alla^h warns you against Himself (His Punishment), and to Alla^h is the final return." Also see Sura 60:1, 4:144, 5:51, 8:73.

In other words, Muslims can outwardly pretend to be your friends, to guard against you, to strengthen themselves against you. Some Muslims will argue that this is only in Shi'a Islam, but Ibn Kathir, a highly regarded Sunni scholar, records, as an argument for Taqiyya, "We smile in the face of some people although our hearts curse them" (Fath Al Bāri, 10:544, quoted in Ibn Kathir, *Tafsir Vol.* 2, p. 141–43). He also argues that Muslims can even deny that they are Muslims and deny Islam, the Qur'an, and Muhammad, in the interest of self preservation. They can lie to promote a social "good" (i.e., promote Islam) (Imamovic, *Outlines of Islamic Doctrine*, p. 346). As such, treaties are not binding (Sura 47:35; 2:224–225; 66:1–2; 16:91, 94) and used to provide time to regroup and rearm. Ghazali, the most famous and highly regarded Muslim scholar of all times, states that lying is obligatory when the goal is obligatory, and it cannot be reached by telling the truth (Ahmad ibn Naqib al-Misri, (1368), *Reliance of the Traveller*, translated by Nuh

Ha Mim Keller (1994), r. 8.2, p. 745). Dawah (Islamic evangelism) is obligatory; if Islam cannot be spread with the truth, they are obliged to lie. According to Ghazali, Muhammad taught people to retract truthful confessions of sins so they could avoid punishment; lying is also permissible if the consequences of telling the truth are more damaging than the damage by lying (ibid., p. 746).

The ultimate purpose of Taqiyya is to confuse and split the enemy, so that they can be conquered for Allah. A perfect example of this is when Sura 2:256 is quoted, "there is no compulsion in religion," but they fail to cite Sura 9:5, 29 (and others) which abrogate 2:256. Today, unbelievers only have the choice of converting, paying protection money, or facing humiliation by Muslims or death. On the one hand, the Qur'an in numerous places condemns falsehood, but as we have seen, not only do Allah and Muhammad practice lying, but Muhammad also taught his followers how to lie and deceive. Unfortunately for Muslims, the long history of lying has caused many Muslims to believe their own lies. Irshad Manji, *The Trouble with Islam* (Sydney: Random House, 2003), p. 3.

Truth in the Bible

The Bible teaches the exact opposite. It does not condone or allow for deceit of any kind (Revelation 22:15). Believers are commanded to keep their oaths even to their own detriment (Joshua 9, Psalm 15:4). In fact, Yahweh, the God of the Bible, says that He is not a man, that He would not lie (Number 23:19). The Bible describes Jesus as Truth (John 14:6), the Holy Spirit as Truth (1 John 5:6), and the Father has not the slightest deceit in Him (James 1:17; 2 Samuel 7:28; Psalm 31:5). Jesus *is* truth. Believers are to be Holy as God is Holy (Leviticus 19:2; 1 Peter 1:16, etc.). In the New Testament period, the seriousness of sin and lying was highlighted when God killed some people who lied (Acts 5). The Bible declares, "All liars will have their part in the lake which burns with fire and brimstone" (Revelation 21:8 NKJV).

However, in Islam, if you do not sin, Allah will kill you and replace you with people who will sin (Muslim, Book 37, Hadith No. 6622, 6621). We have brought you this message because we love you and desire to see you know the truth; we want you to know that you can have your mind, body, heart, and soul cleansed by Jesus.

APPENDIX 2

Allah, the God of the Qur'an versus Yahweh, the God of the Bible

As I mentioned in my story, I was born into a nominal Christian family. Growing up in Pakistan, studying in Islamic schools, I learned that Allah has ninety-nine names, and those names are because of his character and attributes. Most of those names are like—Creator, All Merciful. We used to think that there was little difference between Christianity and Islam. We thought Christians and Muslims both worship the same god. We call the God of the Bible in my language *Khuda*, which means creator. We understood that Muslims called God Allah. We thought we worshipped the same god. The only difference was that we worshipped Jesus while they worshipped Mohammed. Many Jews, Christians, and Muslims today believe that they are the same God because they have not studied on a deeper level. But after becoming Christian, I discovered that these two gods, the God of the Christians and the god of the Muslims, are not the same. They are totally and completely, absolutely, diabolically opposite. I learned that not anywhere in the Qur'an is Allah called love. In the Holy Bible we quickly learn that God is love. Also, not anywhere in the Qur'an is Allah called father. In fact, it is a blasphemy to say that Allah is my father— actually an unpardonable sin. But, on the other hand, the God of the Bible tells us that we are His children and He is our Father. Praise God! Let me share with you the teachings about what the Qur'an says about Allah and what the Holy Bible says about Yahweh God. I have already learned that I do not worship Allah; I worship Yahweh, the God of the Bible. He is love, and He is my Father. Hallelujah!

Although Christians and Muslims claim the God of Abraham as their own, closer examination reveals that Allah and Yahweh are vastly different. In the Bible and the Qur'an, both Yahweh and Allah respectively are described as Creator, One, Ruler, Revealer, Loving, and Forgiving, and as Judge. The Qur'an claims that Allah and the God of the Bible are identical:

"And argue not with the People of the Scripture unless it be in (a way) that is better, save with such of them as do wrong; and say: We believe in that which has been revealed unto us and revealed unto you; our God and your God is One, and unto Him we surrender." [Pickthall's translation] (Surah 29:46).

In light of this teaching in the Qur'an, Muslims claim that Christians have misrepresented Allah as a threefold God and that they should revert to the original simplicity of the oneness (Tawhid) of Allah.

The Bible is much older than the Qur'an, and numerous proofs exist to show that the Bible has not been changed/tampered with over the centuries, as many Muslims claim. It would be reasonable to expect that what Allah reveals in the Qur'an and what Yahweh reveals in the Bible should be identical; the Qur'an should confirm the facts of the Bible and its teachings. However, a study of the Bible and the Qur'an shows that the apparent similarities mentioned above have very different meanings for each faith.

Below are references, first from the Holy Bible, and then from the Qur'an:

- Yahweh creates only good (Genesis 1, 1 Timothy 4:4, James 1:17).

Allah creates good and evil (Surah 4:78, 113:2).

- Yahweh loves all mankind (John 3:16).

Allah loves Muslims (Surah 2:195, 2:190, 2:276, 3:32).

- Yahweh does not change (Malachi 3:6, James 1:17).

Allah changes his mind frequently (Surah 16:101, 13:39, 17:86, 87:6–8).

- Yahweh guarantees heaven for believers (John 6:47, 10:27–28; Romans 6:23; 1 John 5:11–13).

Allah guarantees hell for a time for believers (Surah 19:71–72).

- Yahweh does not lie; He stands by His promises (Numbers 23:19, 1 Samuel 15:29).

Allah lies when convenient (Surah 3:54, 8:30).

- Yahweh leads people in the path of life (Psalm 23, 139:24; John 14:6).

Allah leads astray whom he wills (Surah 7:178–79, 13:31, 95:4–5, 4:142, 39:57, 18:17).

- Yahweh is a complex unity: infinity+infinity+infinity=infinity (John 10:30, 14:9; Romans 8:9–11).

Allah is one unity (Surah 4:171, 5:73).

- Yahweh demands eternal justice (Psalm 37:28; Isaiah 30:18, 42:1–4, 61:8, 65:6; Jeremiah 9:24; Ezekiel 18:4; Matthew 16:27).

Allah doesn't demand eternal justice (Surah 7:8, 21:47, 23:101–103, 53:32, 5:39, 11:114; Bukhari, Vol. 1, Hadith No. 17, 50453, etc).

- Yahweh always forgives believers (Colossians 2:13, 1 John 1:9).

Allah forgives believers when he pleases (Surah 2:284, 3:129, 4:48, and 116).

- Yahweh has a son (Psalm 2; Proverbs 30:4; Matthew 3:17, 17:5).

Allah does not have a son (Surah 112:3–4, 72:1–5, 19:92).

- Yahweh provides atonement and intercession (Deuteronomy 32:43, Isaiah 53:12, Romans 8:34, Hebrews 7:25).

Allah many times refuses atonement and intercession (Surah 2:186; 6:51, 94; 10:18; 32:4; 19:95).

- Yahweh hates sin (Romans 3:25; 1 John 2:2, 4:10; Numbers 19:1–2; Exodus 19:6; Psalm 119:142, 160; Matthew 5:48; 1 Peter 1:15–16).

Allah demands sin (Muslim, Book 37, Hadith No. 6622, 6621; Book 33, Hadith No. 6421).

- Yahweh is a personal God (Jeremiah 24:7, 31:34; John 10:14, 14:9; Romans 8:15; Galatians 4:6; Revelation 21:7).

Allah is unknowable and impersonal, a master of slaves (Surah 4:172, 5:118, 6:18, 7:194, 15:49, 19:93).

Indeed, as you can see from the Biblical and Qur'anic references above, the character of Yahweh God is very different from the described character of Allah.

Allah Has No Son; Yahweh Has a Son

The Bible states that God is triune: Father, Son, and Holy Spirit. The concept of a triune God is a difficult one to understand. While a mathematical formula would tell us that 1+1+1=3, that does not explain the trinity. Rather, it is a complex unity more like: infinity + infinity + infinity = infinity. As Christians, we do not worship three gods, and we consider it blasphemy to suggest that we do.

Muslims draw their understanding of the Trinity from the Qur'an (Sura 4:171, 5:116, 21:91, 66:12). It would seem that Mohammed evidently heard about the Trinity from Christian heretics rather than from the Gospels (*Injil*) themselves (Matthew 28:19).

Perhaps the biggest and most critical difference is that Allah denies having a son, and will not forgive people who say that he does (Sura 5:17, 72; 3:61; 9:31).

By contrast, Yahweh God does have a Son. His name is Jesus Christ. It is through the Son Jesus that we become children of Yahweh God. (John 1:12, 14:6–9; Galatians 3:26, 4:4–7; Hebrews 1:1–2; 1 John 5:1; Revelation 21:7) and have eternal life. Jesus being called the Son of God is referring to His eternal intimate relationship with the Father, Yahweh God.

Allah vs. Yahweh God on the Forgiveness of Sin

Mohammed prayed frequently for the forgiveness of his sins, but there was no assurance that his sins were forgiven or that he would go to heaven (Sura 46:9; Bukhari, Vol. 8, Hadith No. 319). This is understandable since Allah does not always forgive sin (Sura 2:284; 3:129; 4:48, 116).

By contrast, Yahweh God tells us through His Word, "If we confess our sins, He is faithful and just, to forgive us **our** sins and cleanse us from all unrighteousness." (1 John 1:9 NKJV).

Yahweh God is described as a just and holy God (Psalm 51) who punishes all sin because, ultimately, sin is against God (Numbers 15:31). In fact, from Yahweh's perspective, if you have broken just one law, you have broken all of the law (James 2:10) because you have despised God and put yourself in His place as ruler of your life. Thus, unlike Allah (Sura 53:32; 5:39; 11:114; Bukhari, Vol. 1, Hadith No. 17, 504), Yahweh does not allow punishment or good deeds in this life to substitute for punishment in the next (Revelation 21:8).

Jesus Christ died to pay the penalty for our sins once and for all. He rose again on the third day victorious over death, but each one of us must choose to receive this free gift. If you refuse to receive this gift, you cannot enjoy the benefits of the gift. Yahweh God desires us to humbly receive this gift with a thankful heart. *If you wish to receive the forgiveness of sin through Jesus Christ by faith, you need only to open your heart and ask God in your own words.* (Refer to chapter 13 in this book.)

APPENDIX 3

Deception versus Truth

As you read in my story, because of being born in a poor, nominally Christian family, I lived in a culture of shame. Shame is considered a big thing, and guilt is almost ignored. In that culture, we become very good at hiding things because we don't want to be ashamed—it is a matter of our name, our family name—concern for what people will think about us. I want to share with you that I was truly ashamed of my past behavior and regret it. I lived a double life. But, I am no longer ashamed because the Bible tells me that those who are in Christ Jesus have no condemnation. I am a new creation in God through Jesus Christ. I am a new man, washed with the blood of Jesus Christ. My sins are forgiven and forgotten by Almighty God. And now I can say that I am a holy man of God because of the blood of Jesus Christ, and the righteousness which He obtained for me by dying on the cross at Calvary, carrying my sins to the cross. Now I am free from shame and guilt. My past, present, and future are washed and cleansed with the blood of my Lord Jesus Christ. I am destined for eternal life in and through and with my Lord Jesus Christ. I am eternally saved. My name is written in the Lamb's Book of Life. I praise Jesus. He did it all for me. Now I am free from the power of sin and deception, through the power of the blood of Jesus Christ and the Holy Spirit who dwells in me. Every day, I am becoming more and more like Jesus. There was no deceit—there is no deceit found in Him! By God's grace, and through the power of the Holy Spirit and the power of the blood of Jesus, and through the power of His Word, sin no longer rules in my life. I am no longer a slave to sin, but to righteousness.

As I share with you about the deception found in Islam, I am not criticizing Muslims. I love them very much, and I truly pray that they will learn the Truth. The Bible says, "You shall know the Truth and the Truth shall make you free" (John 8:32 NKJV). Jesus Christ is the Truth and the only Truth. I pray that just as the Lord Jesus Christ has set me free, Muslims throughout the earth will also be set free from the power of sin and deception. The information provided on these pages is not to condemn Muslims, but to educate you. My desire is that as you understand the deception that has kept them in bondage, you will pray for these lost souls. Let us read what the Qur'an, Hadith, and Islamic writings say about sin and deception. As you read, do not read in order to use this information as a bomb against Muslims. Rather, read with prayer and compassion, with the intention of understanding—and with the desire to see them walk free in Christ.

Throughout the Holy Bible, a consistent standard of righteousness is reflected. Again and again, the writers of the Bible emphasize truth. Jesus said in John 14:6 (NKJV), "I am the Way, the TRUTH and the Life. No one comes to the Father except through Me." And, John 8:32 (NKJV) tells us, "And you shall know the truth and the truth shall make you free."

Repeatedly, Yahweh tells His people in His Word to trust Him because He is a covenant-keeping, faithful God (Genesis 17:7; Exodus 34:6; Deuteronomy 7:9; Psalm 36:5, 89:33; 2 Timothy 2:13; Hebrews 13:20).

Yahweh's Word stands forever and does not change (Isaiah 40:8, Matthew 24:35, Luke 21:33, Numbers 23:19, Malachi 3:6).

In contrast, when we read the Qur'an, we discover that Allah abrogates or changes his words (Sura 28:59, 16:101, 13:39, 17:86, 87:6–8). It is difficult to trust a god who changes his preferred people, his methodology or standards.

Allah does as he pleases, leading people in the right way or leading them astray. Sura 3:54: "And they cheated/deceived and God cheated/deceived, and God (is) the best (of) the cheaters—deceivers. (Translated by Mohamed Ahmed and Samira Ahmed) (See also Sura 8:30.) The word used in Suras 3:54 and 8:30, *makara*, means to deceive, delude, cheat, double-cross, and dupe. Allah is thus seen as the best of deceivers, the premier schemer, and the conniving one. By contrast, Isaiah, speaking of Yahweh, says that there is no deceit in God's mouth (Isaiah 53:9).

APPENDIX 4

Salvation in Islam

Growing up in Pakistan, we were told that there are only three religions that worship one god: Jews, Christians, and Muslims. We were taught all three would go to heaven, but the Qur'an later explains that Jews corrupted the Torah so they have been rejected and will not go to heaven. The Qur'an also says that Christians changed the Gospel (*Injil*), so they cannot enter heaven either. So now, according to the Qur'an, God's chosen people are Muslims. They are the only ones who will go to paradise. In Islam, heaven is where Allah dwells. Muslims will not be in heaven—in the presence of their god. But, the appeal of paradise is very great because of the pleasures awaiting them. Actually the writings of Islam on paradise and heaven are conflicting in that some refer to paradise and heaven as separate and other writings refer to them as one and the same.

After becoming a Christian, I really began to study the Qur'an, the Hadith, and the Islamic classical writings. I discovered that there is no place in the Qur'an where anyone is guaranteed that they will go to heaven. The concept of salvation is so confused that even Mohammed, the prophet of Islam, did not know whether he would go to heaven. So let's look at some of the writings of the Qur'an and Hadith, and other writings, to learn what they say about salvation in Islam.

Actually all Muslims go to hell when they die. However, after some time they will be released and go to paradise. The time they remain in hell is dependent upon the kinds of sins they committed. Only those who believe in Jesus Christ will remain there.

Christianity teaches that there is a broken relationship between God and mankind that needs restoration. Any soul that sins shall die in the lake of fire. The only way to avoid that is to trust in the atonement of Christ. In Christianity, the only sinless one, the Son of God, Jesus Christ, was given as that atonement:

"This is love, not that we loved God, but that He loved us and sent His Son to be the propitiation for our sins" (1 John 4:10 NKJV).

"If any man sin, we have an advocate with the Father, Jesus Christ the righteous, and He is the propitiation for our sins, and not for ours only, but also for the sins of the whole world" (1 John 2:1–2 KJV).

Islam offers guidance but not salvation. In Islam, there is no relationship with Allah, so there is no broken relationship, and so no need for a mediator. Atonement is something you do to atone for sin (such as broken, intentional oaths, having sex during a fast, etc.), usually a "payment" of some nature, including punishment imposed by others who caught you in your sin. Thus atonement is limited to this world, so if you are punished now, or provide your own atonement via some payment, Allah will not punish you in the hereafter (Bukhari, Vol. 1, Hadith No. 17; Muslim, Vol. 3, Hadith No. 4235). For a sinless, innocent prophet like Jesus [Isa] to atone for your sin is an insult to Allah and is forbidden in the Qur'an (Sura 4:112, 17:15, etc.). Thus, whereas the God of the Bible guarantees salvation, Allah saves who he wills. In fact, Allah guarantees that every Muslim will pass through hell (Sura 19:71–72).

In Christianity, you cannot truly follow God unless *He* has changed what is in your heart (Mark 7:21–23, Ezekiel 36:26). In Islam, you cannot truly follow Allah, until *you* change your *own* heart (Sura13:11).

Heaven, to a Christian, is to be with Jesus. While an actual place, the Christian cherishes the fact that it is with Jesus they spend eternity. In the Christian Heaven, there is no sin or sinner. The lake of fire is reserved for Satan and his angels, and unbelievers (Matthew 25:31–46). Islamic Heaven (Paradise), has seventy-two virgins for the lowliest person (Sura 56:22–40, Ibn Kathir on 56:22–40). There will be free-flowing wine in abundance (Sura 56:18; 76:5, 17; 78:34). Demons [*Jinn*] will also be in Paradise (Ibn Kathir, commenting on Sura 55:56–74).

APPENDIX 5

What Is Jihad?

After completing my high school studies, I went to college, where I began premed studies, hoping to become a medical doctor. At the same time, the government of Pakistan offered a National Guard training program. This program would help me to gain admission to medical school more easily than with my education alone. When I completed my premed studies, I would also be completing my National Guard training. I would have two certificates in my hands. I did join, and the training was great, as they taught us all the military exercises. They also instilled in our hearts patriotism and intensified commitment to the Muslim faith. They emphasized that the reward for dying in Jihad was the assurance of going to paradise and all the promises that were waiting for us there.

I had already studied the Qur'an and learned about Jihad, but there was no opportunity for us to participate. But through the national training, I began to see the possibilities—the dream of serving our country and our faith, leaving a wonderful legacy and receiving great benefits—going to paradise and being the recipient of seventy-two virgins!

The concept of dying in Jihad is that you are shedding your own blood to be your own sacrifice—ensuring your ticket to paradise. That is one major reason that when a Muslim is killed in Jihad, they don't wash the body, but rather bury the person in the clothes he/she was wearing, stained with the blood. The belief is that when he stands before the gate of paradise, the gate will be opened because of his own blood sacrifice.

I have learned as a Christian that that does not work! When Adam and Eve sinned against God, we inherited the sinful nature. The Holy Bible tells us that "all have sinned and come short of the glory of God" (Romans 3:23 KJV). So there is no way that I can purchase or earn my salvation. In order for me to be free from the power of sin, I need the sacrifice of something that is sinless. I cannot find anything or anyone in this world that is not under the power of sin or that curse. Because of Adam's and Eve's sins, everything came under the curse—trees, animals, everything. So, there is no way anyone can find anything to be his or her sacrifice for the redemption of sins.

God sent His Son to die, the only acceptable sacrifice. Because of His sinless life and sinless blood, He is the only acceptable sacrifice. The door of heaven will not open with my own good deeds or even with my own blood because my good deeds are like filthy rags in the sight of the Holy and Almighty God. And my blood is a sinful blood. I will enter heaven only through the righteousness of my Lord Jesus Christ and through His blood. The door of heaven is opened through the blood of Jesus Christ, not through my own or any other beings'. I can see for myself, there is nothing good in me.

As you are reading this book, if you think you are good enough, examine your life in the light of the Ten Commandments and ask yourself—"Have I ever broken any of these commandments?" "Have I ever told a lie?" "Have I ever committed adultery?" Jesus said that even if you look at a woman with a lustful eye, you have committed adultery. If you go through the list, you will find that we have broken almost all of those commandments. And even if you have broken only one, according to the book of James, you have broken them all.

You and I deserve to be burning in hell because there is nothing good in us that can qualify us to go to heaven, and our blood is sinful blood. It is not going to open the door for us in heaven. The only answer, what we really need, is the righteousness of God through Christ Jesus and the remission of our sins through the blood of Jesus Christ. As you read, I humbly ask that if you have not asked Jesus Christ to be your Lord and Savior, please ask Him now. Let His blood become your sacrifice that you may go to heaven and have eternal life. "The next day he saw Jesus coming toward him and said, 'Behold! The Lamb of God who takes away the sin of the world!'" (John 1:29 NKJV). Jesus died on the cross for you, for your sins and my sins. He shed his blood for you and for me. He died and was buried. But, hallelujah, He rose on the third day, overcoming death and the grave.

Let me explain to you how the Qur'an and the Hadith and other Islamic writings explain Jihad and Islamic martyrdom, and their belief that it is through dying in Jihad that they have their "ticket to paradise."

Islamic terrorists claim their authority from the Qur'an and Mohammed's life—though "moderate" Muslims claim that such teachings are not found in Islam, or are a misunderstanding of the texts. It is important to evaluate the claims of both of these groups. The best way to evaluate the authenticity of a religion or practice is to examine the teachings, the life, and the practice of its founder—in this case, Mohammed.

Teachings of Mohammed

According to Ibn Is'haq 326, "Allah said, 'No Prophet before Mohammed took booty from his enemy nor prisoners for ransom.' Mohammed said, 'I was made victorious with terror. The earth was made a place for me to clean. I was given the most powerful words. Booty was made lawful for me. I was given the power to intercede. These five privileges were awarded to no prophet before me.'"

When Mohammed was in a weak and needy position, he advocated peace. But, when he had money, an army, and was in a position of power, he planned and fought at least sixty-seven wars against Christians, Jews, and others.

A cursory examination of the explanations of Islamic terrorists almost invariably shows that they are motivated by Jihad—a holy war against unbelievers (infidel or *kafir*). Many will argue that *Jihad* means "self-struggle," but as Walid Shoebat, a former Islamic terrorist, now Christian, puts it, "so does '*Mein Kampf*,' by Adolf Hitler."

There are many verses in the Qur'an that convey the impression that Allah and Mohammed are peace-loving. However, the majority of these come from the Meccan period, when Islam (Mohammed) was in a position of weakness. The later teachings are far more violent, the most famous of which are Sura 9:5 and 9:29—known as "the Sword verses":

"Then, when the sacred months have passed, **slay the idolaters wherever you find them**, and take them (captive), and besiege them, and prepare for them each ambush. But if they repent and establish worship and pay the poor-due, then leave their way free. Lo! Allah is Forgiving, Merciful" (Sura 9:5).

"**Fight against those who believe not (1) in Allah**, (2) nor in the Last Day, (3) nor forbid that which has been forbidden by Allah and His Messenger (4) and those who acknowledge not the religion of truth (i.e., Islam) among the people of the Scripture (Jews and Christians), until they pay the Jizyah with willing submission, and feel themselves subdued" (Sura 9:29).

Noted Islamic scholar Anwar ul Haqq, in his book *Abrogation in the Qur'an*, has identified **more than one hundred verses abrogated by these two**—such as:

"There is no compulsion in religion" (Sura 2:256).

"Revile not those unto whom they pray beside Allah lest they wrongfully revile Allah through ignorance. Thus unto every nation have we made their deed seem fair. Then unto their Lord is their return, and He will tell them what they used to do" (Sura 6:108).

"Keep to forgiveness (O Mohammed), and enjoin kindness, and turn away from the ignorant" (Sura 7:199).

"Tell those who believe, to forgive those who do not look forward to the Days of Allah: It is for Him to recompense (for good or ill) each People according to what they have earned" (Sura 45:14).

"Unto you your religion, and unto me my religion" (Sura 109:6).

As Mohammed grew in power, he began to teach that if Muslims do not engage in Jihad, they will go to hell and suffer a painful doom (Sura 48:16–17, 9:81, 9:94–95). Paradise is promised for those who die for Allah (Sura 3:157–58). True Muslims take part in Holy War (Sura 49:15, 9:44). There are said to be as many as 480 exhortations for Jihad in the Qur'an. Here are but a few:

"Warfare is ordained for you, though it is hateful unto you; but it may happen that you hate a thing which is good for you, and it may happen that you love a thing which is bad for you. Allah knows, you know not" (Sura 2:216).

"Allah said, '**A prophet must slaughter before collecting captives**. A slaughtered enemy is driven from the land. Mohammed, you craved the desires of this world, its goods and the ransom captives would bring. But Allah desires killing them to manifest the religion'" (Sura 8:67).

"Those who believe in Allah and the Last Day ask no leave of you lest they should strive with their wealth and their lives. Allah is Aware of those who keep their duty (unto Him)" (Sura 9:44).

"Those who believed and left their homes and strove for the cause of Allah, and those who took them in and helped them—these are the believers in truth. For them is pardon, and bountiful provision" (Sura 8:74).

"The (true) believers are those only who believe in Allah and His messenger and afterward doubt not, but strive [take part in Jihad] with their wealth and their lives for the cause of Allah. Such are the sincere" (Sura 49:15).

"Those who believe do battle for the cause of Allah; and those who disbelieve do battle for the cause of idols. So fight the minions of the devil. Lo! the devil's strategy is ever weak" (Bukhari Vol. 1, Hadith No. 24), 'Narrated Ibn Umar': Allah's Messenger said: "**I have been ordered (by Allah) to fight against the people until they testify that none has the right to be worshipped but Allah and that Mohammed is Allah's Messenger)**" (Sura 4:76).

According to Sura 2:217, "to turn men away from Allah is worse than killing. So killing an infidel who turns people away from Islam is permitted at any time."

Furthermore, Timridhi's Hadith 402 says, "the Prophet (peace be upon him and grant him peace) said: A martyr does not suffer when he is slain any more than one of you suffers from being bitten by an ant." Mohammed himself wanted over and over again to be martyred, according to Bukhari, Vol. 1, Hadith No. 35. Note also Bukhari, Vol. 4, Hadith No. 220, which says, 'Allah's apostle said, "I have been made victorious through terror."'

In al-Tabari IX, p. 42: An unbeliever, 'Amr b. Umayyah said, "We have been dealt a situation from which there is no escape. You have seen what Mohammed has done. Arabs have submitted to him and we do not have the strength to fight. **You know that no herd is safe from him. And no one even dares go outside for fear of being terrorized**."

These are just a small sampling of passages from the Qur'an. Mohammed personally led more than twenty-seven battles in nine years (Ibn Kathir, *Albedayah wa-Nehayah,* Vol. 4, p. 179). There are hundreds more verses that show that Mohammed was a practitioner of what he preached—violent Jihad for Allah.

By contrast, as we observe the teachings of Jesus we note immediately that sinners flocked to Him, and loved to be near Him. They had no fear of death from Him. It is true that Jesus did say, "Do not think that I came to bring peace to the earth. I did not come to bring peace, but a sword" (Matthew 10:34 NKJV). However, he was referring to Christians becoming victims of the sword of godless men. When a disciple on one occasion used a sword to attack Jesus's enemies, Jesus actually healed the injured man and rebuked his disciple (Luke 22:49–51).

Whereas Mohammed sought to force unbelievers to submit, Jesus sought to conquer men's hearts. Jesus said, "My kingdom is not of this world. If My kingdom were of this world, My servants would fight, so that I should not be delivered to the Jews; but now My kingdom is not from here" (John 18:36 NKJV). Jesus taught his disciples "not to resist even an evil person" (Matthew 5:39 NKJV), "to bless those who persecute you; to bless and do not curse" (Romans 12:14 NKJV), and to love your enemies and pray for those who persecute you (Matthew 5:44 NKJV).

The message of Allah/Mohammed and the message of Jesus are the complete opposite. Mohammed offered no assurance of salvation, only the possibility of Allah's mercy, while Jesus died to offer salvation for you as a free *gift* of God; it is not something you can earn. Ephesians 2:8–9 (NASB) says, "It is by grace you (have been) saved, through faith—and that not of yourselves; it is the gift of God, not as a result of works, so that no one may boast."

APPENDIX 6

Women in Islam

You may have seen on television or in movies that there are only Muslim men praying in the mosques. So the question is where are the women? Are they not allowed to worship their god, side by side with their husbands, fathers, and brothers? What is going on? Why are they not in that worship place?

Sometimes we see Muslim women in the market here in the United States. Sometimes they are wearing a scarf, and others are covered from head to toe in long robe-like attire. You might wonder what is going on. Let me tell you what I was taught when I was growing up in Pakistan. Because of the influence of the Islamic culture, although I was born into a nominally Christian family, I would say that 90 percent of the things we believed were learned through Islamic teachings. We were told that women are second class. We were told that we should beat our wives on our wedding nights so that they would be submissive. "Women are like shoes—if they fit, great. If they don't fit, taught about women for most of my life was not the teaching of the Holy Bible. Instead what I had learned was coming from the Islamic teachings. In the West, when we say something about the position of women in Islam, we are told, "Oh, that is just happening in those other countries—it is just cultural, not really in the Qur'an." So let's go together on a journey to explore from the Qur'an, Hadith, and the Islamic writings what their sacred books say about women. And then we will look at what the Holy Bible tells us about women.

According to Christian belief, husbands are commanded to "love your wives, even as Christ also loved the church, and gave himself for it" (Ephesians 5:25 KJV). But as people turn away from the Bible, the suffering of women and others increases. Some have claimed biblical our Western culture, irrespective of race, religion or gender, is that:

1. Yahweh, the God of the Bible, created man and woman in His own image and likeness (Genesis 1:27).
2. In Christ, all who accept Him as their Lord and Savior are adopted into His family (John 1:12, Galatians 3:28).
3. God condemns partiality (1 Timothy 5:21, James 3:17).

In Islamic teaching, Allah claims that he created all human beings as his slaves (Sura 19:93), and as such, no one is or can be a child of Allah. As a result, there is no equality of people before Islamic law in the teachings of the Qur'an and Hadith.

Islamic writings have many references to the deficiencies/inequalities of women as compared to men. Here are some of them:

• A woman's witness (in court) is worth half a man's (Sura 2:282; Bukhari Vol. 3, Hadith No. 826).
• Women are deficient in intelligence and religious practices (Bukhari Vol. 1, Hadith No. 301; Vol. 3, Hadith No. 826; Vol. 2, Hadith No. 541).
• Women are referred to as possessions such as gold, silver, horses, and cattle (Sura 3:14).
• A woman is to be used like a field according to the husband's desires (Sura 2:223).
• A man can exchange one of his wives for another (Sura 4:20).
• A woman comes in the form of a devil (Muslim, Vol. 2, Hadith No, 3240).

Here are further statements about women, and declarations about the privileges of men:

- Women will be the majority in hell (Bukhari Vol. 1, Hadith No. 301; also Muslim, Vol. 4, Hadith No. 6600).
- The best of women are neither to be seen by, nor to see, a man (Ghazali quoted this Hadithin Ihya' 'Uloum ed-Din, vol. 2, Kitab Adab al-Nikah. Beirut: Dar al-Kotob al-'Elmeyah, p. 53).
- A man can marry up to four wives (Sura 4:3, 129).
- A man can have a child wife (Sura 65:4 "The Noble Qur'an").
- Men can have temporary wives (Sura 4:24; Bukhari Vol. 7, Hadith No. 13A, 52; Muslim, Vol. 2, Hadith No. 3247; Bukhari, Vol. 6, 139).
- Men are commanded to beat their wives (Sura 4:34).
- A man can have any number of concubines (Sura 70:29–30).
- Men are better than women (Sura 4:34).

The above teachings provide a "license" for Muslim men to oppress women. While it is true that some Christian men oppress their wives, they have no scriptural basis for their actions.

Rape and Adultery

In 1979, Pakistan adopted the Hudood Ordinances, which are essentially Sharia law. These laws almost completely blur the distinction between rape and adultery.

Adultery is proven if a person admits to having sex with someone to whom he/she is not married.

Under this law, non-Muslims cannot testify against Muslims; the witnesses must be adult, male, and Muslim. A woman's testimony is considered to be only half as valuable as the testimony of a Muslim man (Sura 24:4). Consequently, if a woman cannot provide sufficient witnesses to her rape, she is admitting (under law) to adultery.

The Pakistan Human Rights Commission (PHRC) estimates that a rape occurs every eight minutes and that there are more than fifteen hundred honor killings annually.

- The former mufti of Australia, Sheik al Hilali, stated that if woman does not cover herself properly, she is the one at fault if she is raped.

- The Assyrian International News Agency (December 27, 2005) reported that Lebanese Sheik Faiz Mohammed said that women had no one to blame but themselves.

- The Islamic mufti of Denmark and a panel headed by an Egyptian scholar, Sheik Yusaf al-Qaradawi, claimed female rape victims should be punished if they were dressed immodestly when they were raped: "For her to be absolved from guilt, a raped woman must have shown good conduct" (Telegraph, 11 July 2004). Of course, it would be the male court system that would determine proper and improper dress, as well as good versus bad conduct!

- In Indonesia, in 1998, human rights groups documented the testimony of over one hundred Chinese women who were gang raped during the riots that proceeded the fall of President Suharto. Many of them were told, "You must be raped, because you are Chinese and non-Muslim." This is in accordance with Sura 33:59, "O Prophet! Tell … the believing women, that they should cast their outer garments over their persons (when abroad): that is most convenient, that they should be known (as such) and not molested" (Yusuf Ali's translation).

At one time, Mohammed ordered a man who had committed adultery be given lashes. But, the woman involved was to be stoned to death (Bukhari, Vol. 3, Hadith No. 860).

Jesus tells men that if they so much as look at a woman with lust, they are guilty of adultery (Matthew 5:28). Christian men are also told to treat younger women as their sisters and older women as their mothers (1 Timothy 5:2).

The Veil

In Saudi Arabia in March 2002, fifteen girls died and more than forty others were injured at the Girls' Intermediate School No. 31 in Mecca, the holiest city in Islam. The girls were locked inside when an accidental fire started. The firefighters tried to open the doors but were prevented by the *muttawa* (religious police), who would not let the girls outside the building without their veils (*Newsweek*, July 22, 2002)!

The Qur'an (Sura 24:31) says "that they (women) should lower their gaze and guard their modesty; that they should not display their beauty and ornaments except what (must ordinarily) appear thereof; that they should draw their veils over their bosoms and not display their beauty except to their husbands." Mohammed, the prophet of Allah, told Asma, the daughter of Abu Bakr, that when girls enter the age of menstruation, they must cover themselves, excepting their hands and face (Abu Dawud, Vol 3, Hadith No. 4092).

Marriage

Bukhari Vol. 7, Hadith No. 17: "When I got married, Allah's Apostle said to me, 'What type of lady have you married?' I replied, 'I have married a matron' ... Allah's Apostle said, 'Why didn't you marry a young girl so that you might play with her and she with you?'"

- Mohammed said that the silence of a virgin indicates that she wants to marry (Bukhari Vol. 7, Hadith No. 67).
- Ayatollah Khomeini said that marrying a girl before menstruation was a "divine blessing" and that girls should be married before they menstruate (Taheri, 1986, p. 90–91).
- Mohammed married a six-year-old girl (Bukhari, Vol. 7, Hadith No. 64) and had many wives.

Some say that temporary wives are forbidden in Islam, but Mohammed permitted temporary marriage when his warriors needed them (Sura 4:24; Bukhari, Vol. 7, Hadith No. 51). The first caliph continued to allow temporary marriages. The second caliph forbade the practice, but the last "rightly guided" caliph again allowed temporary marriages. The price (dowry) of a temporary marriage is two handfuls of dates or flour (Abu Dawud, Vol. 2, Hadith No. 2105).

Additional References

Women, dogs, and donkeys can annul the prayers of a man, according to Bukhari, Vol. 1, Hadith No. 490 and 493. But the Bible says that husbands are to honor their wives and, if they are angry with their wives, their prayers will not be heard (1 Peter 3:7).

Mohammed's most beloved wife, Aisha, said "O womenfolk, if you knew the rights that your husbands have over you, every one of you would wipe the dust from her husband's feet with her face." [M. Al-Hashimi, *The Ideal Muslimah*, (1996), chapter 4].

Mohammed taught that, "God permits you to shut them [your wives] in separate rooms and to beat them, but not severely. Treat women well, for they are (like) domestic animals (*awan*) with you and do not possess anything for themselves." (*The History of al-Tabari*, volume IX, p. 113.)

Christians have a completely different view of the value and rights of a woman. The Holy Bible says that in Jesus Christ, there is neither male nor female, slave nor free (Galatians 3:28). All believers have equal value and rights because men and women are made in the image of God (Genesis 1:27, 5:2).

- Husbands are commanded to: love their wives as Jesus loves the Church and died for her (Ephesians 5:25 NKJV), not to be angry with or harsh with them (Colossians 3:19), love their wives as their own bodies (Ephesians 5:28, 33 NKJV), and to be kind to their wives (1 Corinthians 7:3–5 NKJV). There is not a single command that suggests or encourages a husband to beat or be harsh with his wife.

- Husbands and wives are commanded to submit to one another in Christ (Ephesians 5:21), but husbands must provide for their wives (1 Timothy 5:8).
- Husband and wife are considered to be one flesh before God (Ephesians 5:31); as such, God "hates divorce" (Malachi 2:16 NKJV).

The treatment of men and women in the Bible and Qur'an are completely different. The content here will probably have raised some questions in your mind. Muslims are commanded not to read and believe the Scriptures that God gave Christians and Jews. They are told that the holy books of the Christians and Jews have been corrupted. (Sura 6:115, 10:64–65, 18:27, 48:23).

APPENDIX 7

Information about Pastor Masih

1. Pastor Masih has studied Islam and the Qur'an for many years in Pakistan.
2. Jesus Christ found Pastor Masih and used him to start churches in Pakistan. Now there are over three hundred churches, two Bible schools, and a child-support program in Pakistan; 103 churches in India; thirty-five church-run Bible schools in Sri Lanka; one church in South Africa; a few churches in Rwanda and Uganda; and some work in Dubai, United Arab Emirates. Everything is going to be growing, and more countries throughout the world will be added. Praise God!
3. He has traveled to forty-six states here in the United States of America, and has spoken in over one thousand churches of all sizes.
4. Pastor Masih has also spoken at *Focus on the Family* in Colorado Springs; Pastor John Piper's church in Minneapolis, Minnesota; the national conference for The Voice of the Martyrs; and many regional conferences.
5. Pastor Masih has spoken on Christian television programs, Moody Radio, American Family, and other radio programs.
6. Pastor Masih has given many conferences and seminars on Islam throughout the country.
7. Pastor Masih has also spoken in public and Christian schools, community colleges, Christian colleges and universities such as Colorado Christian University, Biola, Masters College, Denver

Seminary, NCU, University of Colorado Boulder, University in Missoula in Montana, Yavapai College, and many others.

8. Pastor Masih is also an author of a book, *The Fearless Love in Midst of Terror.*

All glory belongs to Jesus, for He made everything possible.

Pastor M. El Masih's vision for the church in the United States of America and for the Muslim world:

Pastor Masih deeply loves the Lord Jesus Christ and the Holy Bible, the Word of God. Pastor Masih also loves the United States of America very much; he is grateful for the freedom found in this country, for there is no freedom of religion in his native country or in any Muslim country around the world. This is why he likes to say, **"I love the USA 200 percent."**

Pastor Masih has suffered through much persecution in his native country, where Muslims burned his town. In this attack, fifteen hundred Christian homes and thirteen church buildings were burned by the Muslims. Although this was a very hurtful event, he has no anger or bitterness toward Muslims. He says, "I love Muslims, and my prayer for them is that they will come to know Jesus Christ as their Lord and Savior." He wants to see the church in the United States of America stand strong and firm for Christ Jesus in spite of persecutions that may arise.

The Bible states in John 8:32: "And ye shall know the truth, and the truth shall make you free." The Word of God also states in Hosea 4:6: "My people are destroyed for lack of knowledge." Therefore, it is imperative for people to know and understand the truth about Islam.

You can find more about Pastor Masih on:
- www.persecutedchristians.org
- www.fortheloveofmuslims.org
- YouTube Channel: Cry of the Persecuted Church

For more information, please call Cry of the Persecuted Church at 402–230–8062.

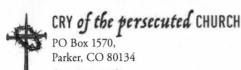

CRY *of the persecuted* CHURCH

PO Box 1570,
Parker, CO 80134
402–230–8062
pastorelmasih@gmail.com

Dear friends of the Persecuted Church,

Please allow us to introduce you to Pastor M El Masih.

In 1997, a Christian believer in Pakistan was falsely accused of tearing a few pages from a single copy of the Quar'an and throwing them "disrespectfully" into a Muslim mosque. Thousands of Muslims were incited to riot at this perceived outrage and stormed two Christina villages in the area. Dozens of churches were destroyed, fifteen hundred houses were burned, and many believers were violated and/or died, all while government officials turned a blind eye.

Pastor Masih, who was living and ministering in the area, survived the attacks and spoke out against the injustice. As a result, he and his family were forced to flee for their lives. God miraculously opened the door for them to come to America, where Pastor Masih has thrived as a popular conference speaker. He is the author of two books: *Fearless Love in the Midst of Terror*, and *Sharing the Gospel with Muslims* (this later book co-authored with Daniel Scot). Pastor Masih speaks excellent English and is a powerful preacher and teacher. He was an associate with Voice of the Martyrs for fifteen years, promoting that organization while speaking on behalf of the persecuted church around the world.

Pastor Masih's primary ministry involves traveling to churches across the United States for weekly conferences and weekend services. In his "spare time," through the ministries he has founded, God has used Pastor Masih to open and operate a pastor training college in Pakistan that has trained hundreds of pastors who have planted hundreds of churches, to also operate a free medical clinic that openly shares the gospel with Muslims, to sustain a wide-ranging child-relief ministry, to establish a ministry that buys the freedom of impoverished Christians working as indentured servants in brick factories, and to launch a ministry that provides bicycles and mopeds for church planters. In addition, Pastor Masih has developed a growing network of partner churches in India, and an exploding network of evangelistic house churches in Sri Lanka.

Please visit the ministry websites and watch several endorsement videos. The ministry websites are: www.persecutedchristians.org and www.fortheloveofmuslims.org .

Pastor Masih is available to speak at your church. To schedule a speaking opportunity, please e-mail him at pastorelmasih@gmail.com, or you may call him at **402–230–8062.**

May the Lord continue to bless your many relationships and responsibilities, and may you be encouraged as you seek to be an encouragement to those suffering for their faith.

From your brothers and sisters at Cry of the Persecuted Church

PERSECUTEDCHRISTIANS.ORG

212

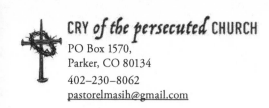

CRY *of the persecuted* CHURCH

PO Box 1570,
Parker, CO 80134
402–230–8062
pastorelmasih@gmail.com

Topics Regarding Islam on Which Pastor Masih Has Spoken Effectively and Often

What is Islam?
1. The origin of Islam
2. Meanings of the word *Islam*
3. The goals of Islam
4. The role of Islam in God's plan for the endtimes
5. Islam and the mark of the beast

What is the Qur'an (The holy book of Islam)?
1. Meanings of the word *Qur'an*
2. Who wrote the Qur'an?
3. When was the Qur'an written?
4. Different names of the Qur'an
5. Stories in the Qur'an that conflict with the Bible
6. Some odd teachings in the Qur'an
7. Does the Qur'an contradict itself?
8. What does the Qur'an teach about Jews and Christians?
9. What does the Qur'an teach about eternal salvation?
10. What is the concept of sin in the Qur'an?

The Life of Mohammed, the "Prophet" of Islam
1. The birth of Mohammed
2. The first marriage of Mohammed
3. Mohammed's call to be The Prophet
4. The goals of Islam
5. Rejection of Mohammed in Makkah (Mecca)

6. Why did Mohammed preach to demons and convert them to Islam?
7. Why did Mohammed declare Jihad on wealthy people?
8. How did Islam spread across Saudi Arabia?
9. The death of Mohammed

Allah. Is He God?
1. Are Allah and the God of the Bible the same god?
2. Who is Allah according to the Qur'an?
3. What is the difference between what Mohammed recorded as being Allah's teaching in the Qur'an versus what Mohammed taught elsewhere?

Why do Muslims Hate Christians and Jews?
1. Teachings in the Qur'an about Jews and Christians.
2. Why does the Qur'an speak positive things about Jews, Christians, and the Bible first, and then say negative things about them later?

What is Jihad according to the Teachings of Islam?
1. Silent Jihad
2. Jihad as self-defense
3. Offensive Jihad
4. Jihad as economic gain
5. Avoidance of Jihad as economic gain
6. Reinforcement of Jihad
7. New revelation of the reinforcement of Jihad
8. Jihad for personal salvation
9. The merit of martyrdom according to the Qur'an
10. Martyrdom according to the Hadith (the sayings of Mohammed)
11. Jihad to spread Islam
12. Jihad against idolaters
13. Jihad against people of the Book (i.e., Jews and Christians)
14. Jihad through the pen
15. Jihad through marriage

16. Jihad through mysticism
17. Jihad with money
18. Mosque
19. Madrassa (Islamic School)

Why Do Muslims Want to Eliminate Jews from the Land of Israel?

Islam's Plan to Take Over America

Sharia, Islamic Law, and Its Threat to America

Islam and the Muslim Brotherhood: How They Are Infiltrating America

Islam and Human Rights

What Does the Qur'an Say about Jews, Christians, the Bible, and Jesus?

What Is the Position of Women in Islam?
1. Male superiority
2. The "deficiencies" of woman
3. A husband's rights
4. A woman's "rights"
5. Male prerogatives
6. The significance of the marriage contract
7. The significance of the dowry
8. The spiritual standing of the woman in Islam

Reaching Muslims for Jesus
1. Prayer, fasting, and spiritual warfare
2. Guidance from the Holy Spirit
3. True knowledge of Islam
4. Miracles
5. Love and hospitality
6. Spiritual boldness

7. Using godly wisdom and not merely knowledge
8. Culture
9. Language
10. Sharing your life-changing experience through Christ Jesus

Teaching on Prayer
1. What is prayer?
2. Why should we pray?
3. Why does God want us to pray?
4. Why is prayer important to God?
5. Principles of prayer.
6. Who can pray?
7. Who cannot pray?
8. What hinders us when we pray?
9. Why does prayer not always seem to be answered?
10. How to expand your time in prayer.
11. All the prayers in the Bible.
12. What is the connection between prayer and fasting?
13. Why should we fast?
14. The different kinds of fasting in the Bible.
15. How to pray effectively for lost souls.
16. Spiritual warfare.
17. Power of the blood of Jesus.
18. The armor of God.

If you need more information, please call
402–230–8062

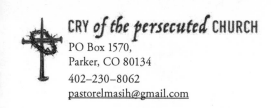

CRY *of the persecuted* CHURCH
PO Box 1570,
Parker, CO 80134
402–230–8062
pastorelmasih@gmail.com

Meeting Guidelines and Suggestions

PRAYER—Please lift up Pastor M El Masih in prayer as he prepares for his time of sharing with you. Pray for his safety in travel and that God would prepare the hearts of those who will be hearing the message.

ARRIVAL—Pastor Masih will arrive at least twenty minutes before the speaking engagement is scheduled to begin, unless otherwise discussed. If the meeting place could be open and a host present to greet him, it would be greatly appreciated.

RESOURCE TABLE—Can you please provide a table—eight feet would be preferable—to display books, videos, and newsletters? If for any reason a table will not be available, please let us know in advance.

VOLUNTEERS—We would appreciate it if you could make someone available to assist Pastor Masih in setting up the resource table beforehand and overseeing it following the meeting. This will enable Pastor Masih to answer questions and visit with people more freely.

FREEWILL OFFERING—Pastor Masih and his family are living by faith. God meets their needs through freewill love offerings, which are taken in church services. These offerings not only pay his expenses but also support a variety of ministries he has established overseas.

Pastor Masih supports over one hundred plus churches in Pakistan, over one hundred in India, an evangelistic medical clinic and two Pastor training Colleges in Pakistan, a number of other Pastor training and support ministries in Dubai, Sri Lanka, South Africa, Rwanda, and Uganda, as well as a variety of support ministries for persecuted

Christians in those countries. The breadth and depth of these ministries is difficult to summarize … all from freewill love offerings.

We do not ask a set fee, but rather request that you take a freewill offering during any of the services at which Pastor Masih is scheduled to speak. Perhaps you could take up your regular tithes and offerings during the first part of the service, and then at the end, you could take up the freewill offering for Pastor Masih. When the offering is to be taken, we would appreciate the congregation being made aware that <u>all checks should be made payable to your church</u>, so that Pastor Masih will receive only one support check from the church. This will greatly help our record keeping. Please make the final check payable to "Cry of the Persecuted Church." If you are not able to have the check ready at the time of the speaking engagement, please mail it to:

CRY of the PERSECUTED CHURCH
PO Box 2570, Parker, CO 80134

If you have any questions about these guidelines and suggestions, please call Pastor Masih at
402–230–8062 or send an e-mail to: pastorelmasih@gmail.com.

Speaker Request Application

Name of Church/School/Organization:
Physical Address:
Mailing Address:
City, State, Zip:
Phone:
Fax:
E-mail:

If Church, name of Pastor:

Name of contact person (if different from pastor):
Mailing address of contact person:
Physical address of contact person:
City, State, Zip:
Phone:
Fax:
E-mail:

Speaking preference date:
Second choice:
Third choice:
Fourth choice:
Time(s) for meeting/service:
Length of meeting/service:
Nature of meeting—(church service, mission conference, school chapel, classroom, home meeting, home school gathering, etc.):
Special topic(s) you would like Pastor Masih to address?

Note: In addition to teaching on Islam or the plight of the persecuted church around the world, Pastor Masih has also taught extensively on a wide variety of other topics, from missions to discipleship, from spiritual warfare to evangelism … just to name a few.

Projected audience size:

Specific audience targeted:

Would you like a biography of the speaker?

Does church have a video projector?

What is appropriate attire for the speaker?

Will your church/organization provide meals and accommodations?

Yes () No ()

*Please be sensitive to the financial responsibilities of hosting a "by faith" speaker. We do not ask a set fee, but rather trust the Lord will cover the expenses

of his through the generosity of your responsive congregation or group.

Is your church/organization willing to take a freewill offering to offset travel expenses and support the ministries of Pastor Masih in the United States and abroad?

Yes [] No. [].

Is your church/organization willing to take up a freewill offering during your church services?

Yes [] No. [].

Please feel free to call or write if you have any questions:

Pastor M El Masih

PO Box 2570

Parker, CO 80134

402–230–8062

pastorelmasih@gmail.com

CRY OF THE *persecuted* CHURCH

An evangelistic crusade sponsored by CPC in India, attended by 15,000 people, of which 10,000 stood up to receive Christ as Savior. 60% were Hindu, 20% Muslim.

P.O. Box 2570, Parker, CO 80134 • persecutedchristians.org

Although it is NOT illegal to discriminate against believers in most Muslim countries, it remains a common practice.

Even in some Buddhist countries like Sri Lanka, where it is illegal to discriminate, the government turns a blind eye. In many Muslim countries, Christians are the poorest of the poor. In smaller cities in Pakistan, they are forced to live in Christian ghettos where most of those believers are only able to work in the lowest paying jobs in their communities. New believers are routinely fired. They are quite often openly persecuted, at times maimed, sexually brutalized, tortured, and sometimes killed. In 1997, Pastor Masih's village was looted: 1500 Christian homes and 13 churches were destroyed, and hundreds of believers brutalized by an angry mob, because of the rumor that a one Christian had torn a few pages from a copy of the Quran (Koran). Sadly, this is not an isolated incident.

But by the grace of God, hardships such as these have only fueled the Church's growth across South Central Asia. Those 13 Pakistani churches destroyed in 1997 have multiplied many times over. The Lord has produced much fruit from their suffering: two Bible colleges and training schools for pastors has been set up there, a free evangelistic medical clinic opened, and a program established to help pay school tuition for the poorest of children, as well as to free indentured slaves from the brick factories, and set them up in small retail kiosk businesses of their own. CPC helps finance the marriages for many of their older daughters. In addition, CPC purchases bicycles or motorbikes for pastors in rural areas.

RECENT MINISTRY OPPORTUNITIES

Pastor Masih has ministered in the nation of South Africa for years. On a trip in the Fall of 2015, he visited Uganda and Rwanda as well. **Details of this trip are available on the CPC website www.persecutedchristians.org under the "Update" tab.** Several significant ministry opportunities presented themselves as a result of this visit. Pastor Masih is now helping to create a Pastor Training School in both Rwanda and Uganda. This will serve the needs of those called to lead, but unable to afford, or even receive the training necessary to pastor effectively. Such training, which is readily available in the West, is virtually non-existent for them. This currently involves weekly Skype courses in biblical studies and practical ministry skills. Pastor Masih is also developing weekly video courses for lay people within a growing number of Ugandan and Rwandan churches as well. These will be made available, not by Skype, but through videos that can be replayed and shared.

And, if wasn't wonderful enough news by itself, God opened another amazing door of opportunity for ministry. Satellite television has made it possible in recent years for Pakistani and Indian peoples to watch programming around the world. There are 50 million Punjabi speakers, 600 million Urdu speakers, and 1 billion Hindi speakers who watch some satellite television every day. Pastor Masih speaks all three of these languages. The Urdu speakers alone live in substantial numbers in 56 countries around the world. We have a ministry partner in South Central Asia who has asked Pastor Masih to develop weekly broadcast videos that will be aired in all three languages twice per week. This means he is **preaching the gospel to over a billion unbelievers every week,** and offering spiritual encouragement to several hundred million believers as well. Praise the Lord!

CPC provides relief in many ways — just one is the ministry it established to purchase impoverished believers out of slavery in the evil brick factory system.

Allow me to explain: In Pakistan, Christians are forced to live in ghettos, isolated from the Muslim community, and only allowed to work in the lowest paying jobs. Whether they experience physical persecution or not all Christians in Pakistan experience financial persecution. When the economy is in decline, Christians are the first to be without work. One of the primary industries throughout Pakistan—one that seems to be almost recession-proof— is brick manufacturing. Wood is scarce and needed for cooking, so everything is built of bricks.

Over the last few decades, Muslim brick factory owners have created an evil system of indentured servitude for out-of-work Christians. "We will give you work when no one else can, and even provide you housing, until you are able to get back on your feet." The housing (in a nearly uninhabitable one-room hovel) is free, but the electricity bill for a single, bare light bulb is $15 per month. A family of four, working 12 hours per day, can make 1000 bricks per week. They are paid $10 for every 1000 bricks made, which means they earn $40 per month... which means almost most half of their income goes for electricity. Even if they go without power, their income is not enough to support them. These families are left with no choice but to borrow on account from the factory owner in order to buy food or pay for other necessities. It becomes a vicious cycle from which they cannot escape because the law supports this system. Until they pay off their debt, which is nearly impossible, they remain in "financial slavery." To make matters worse, their Muslim owners often beat them, rape wives and daughters, and coerce them to become Muslim, with no protection provided by the law. For between $1200 to $1500 dollars, an entire family can have their debt absolved and be set free.

In order to keep these families out of indentured servitude, Cry of the Persecuted Church has purchased land on which we would like to build an apartment complex. The cost for construction is $1500 per single-family unit. These would be available on a rotating basis until a family gets back on its feet. And for an additional $1500, a family can purchase a little business. This "financial stake" would allow them to earn a modest living and a save a little money to protect them from future economic crisis.

CRY *of the persecuted* CHURCH
P.O. Box 2570
Parker, CO 80134

persecutedchristians.org

NAME

ADDRESS

CITY   STATE   ZIP

PHONE   EMAIL

☐ I would like to contribute to the monthly support of either an [ ]Asian pastor or pastor in training, or an [ ]African pastor or pastor in training (please check one). Each month I would like to contribute the following amount:

☐ $25   ☐ $50   ☐ $100   ☐ _____   *100% of your gift will go to this pastor or student.*

☐ I would like to make a one-time gift of $_____. *100% of your gift will go to support a church in South Central Asia.*

☐ I would like to partner with Pastor El Masih in boldly proclaiming the gospel in America and speaking on behalf of the persecuted church in Asia & Africa.

☐ I promise to pray regularly/daily for Pastor El Masih and for the persecuted church in SCA.
☐ Through a one-time gift of $
☐ Through a monthly gift of $

Please be sure to include your e-mail address as this is our most efficient and inexpensive way of communicating prayer needs to you.

BECAUSE OF THESE AND OTHER HARDSHIPS, OUR BROTHERS AND SISTERS IN ASIA AND AFRICA NEED OUR HELP.

Did you know that for as little as $100 per month you could supply the entire living expenses of a Pakistani or Indian pastor and his family, and support their ministry? This same monthly amount can also provide for the tuition, fees, books and living expenses for a student at the Pastor Training School, from which hundreds of pastors have graduated, and through whom hundreds of churches have been planted. Many pastors serve more than one church and travel many miles in between. But by the grace of God, dozens of new pastors are graduating every year, and through their ministries thousands of new believers are being baptized. The need is equally great for pastors serving in the more populous and influential urban settings, where it costs approximately $200 per month to live and serve. But can you imagine a Western missionary living in a Pakistani city on only $200 per month?

Would you prayerfully consider taking on the financial responsibility for one of our pastors in training, or for one of our newly graduating pastors?

As the Church continues to grow in Pakistan and India, there is also the need for financial assistance in the building of churches. The entire building for a church seating 200 people can be built in a village area for approximately $20,000. The approximate cost for such a building in a metropolitan area is about $50,000. But again, can you imagine building a church in the United States for only

$20,000 or $50,000? This is the cost of the average automobile in America. Perhaps God might use you to contribute to the building of such a church!

If you would like to support a pastor or a pastor in training, to contribute to the building of a church, or to provide for one of the many other needs of your brothers and sisters in Pakistan or India, or participate in Pastor Mujahid's teaching ministry here in the United States, please fill out the form on the back and send it to the address listed.

Checks should be made payable to "Cry of the Persecuted Church."

May God richly bless you and reward you for any financial expressions of love God may call you to make.

Cry of the Persecuted Church is a non-profit Christian missionary organization and all gifts to it are tax deductible. To keep administrative costs low, receipts for donations to this ministry are sent out at the end of the fiscal year unless requested otherwise

Recommendation

Pastor M El Masih is one of the greatest men of faith I have had the privilege to know. He not only talks about living by faith; he actually does it. This book describes many wonderful experiences in which he trusted Christ, and He miraculously rescued or provided for him. Though he can no longer return to his native Pakistan, Pastor Masih continues to receive death threats, even in the United States, but has been so anointed that he has led even his enemies to faith.

Pastor Masih was born and raised in Pakistan, a nation whose population exceeds two hundred million and where Islam is the official religion. That country continues to face the problems of terrorism, poverty, illiteracy, and corruption in government. It is worse for believers in Christ who, when they convert, are treated as second-class citizens. It is difficult for them to find work, and if they do, to be paid fair wages. When a Christian starts his or her own business, the Muslim community often boycotts it. Christians in Pakistan face these and other difficulties from birth. This is not only a book about Pastor Masih's experience, but also a textbook on how to reach Muslims for Christ." He explains key differences between Christianity and Islam, and exposes many of the threats and dangers that often accompany the teachings of Islam.

This book will increase your faith, help you better understand spiritual warfare, and demonstrate how to resist the devil, and how to trust in Christ for victory. Pastor Masih learned all these lessons as a Christian in a culture hostile to Christianity. By turning away from the world, its praise and promises, and keeping his eyes instead on Jesus, Pastor Masih, though a very humble man, has become a powerful agent for the gospel.

The devil has tried just about every tactic to destroy Pastor Masih and his ministry ... but to no avail. In this book, you will learn about God's plan to increase your faith—that you might trust in Him in the midst of the most difficult circumstances—and learn the importance of spiritual warfare in achieving victory over the attacks of the Wicked One.

The story of Pastor Masih's faith is a bright light in the midst of a dark and sinful world. As you read the pages of this book, you will learn how he trusted in the miraculous power of Christ to move mountains of opposition, persecution, and discrimination, often not knowing where either money or his next meal would come from, what country to go to, and even who to marry. But one obstacle after another was removed as Pastor Masih trusted in the power of Christ "to meet his every need."

Pastor Masih's story will touch your heart and introduce you to the Almighty One who owns the cattle on a thousand hills and has more power in his "little pinky" than all the powers of Satan and his demonic horde combined. This is the story of a man who seeks to make every decision based on the Bible and the truths found therein. Soon there will be another book coming on his dreams and visions. My prayer for you is that the great faith of Pastor Masih will leap off the pages of this book and encourage your faith as well, and that you will commit yourself to praying for him and his ministry.

Preston T. Bailey, DMin, PhD

Made in the USA
Lexington, KY
28 February 2019